So Dad, How Can I Make Dollars & Sense?

Wealth-Building Insights for When Adulting Begins in EARNest

Always Remember
Ya GoTTA LEARN
To EARN #!

Wes Rutledge

Praise for So Dad, How Can I Make Dollars & Sense?

"As a parent who loves, supports and influences two young adults, I applaud Wes for writing a relevant, insightful, fun and easy-to-understand book that will help young adults create a successful financial path for themselves. A MUST-read for any college student!!"

Tim Long

Corporate Account Manager, The J.R. Simplot Company

"Having been in the financial industry since 1986, and having read many books on investing, I found it refreshing to see how Wes Rutledge brings to the reader a time-proven, simple investment approach that, quite frankly, demystifies the art of successful investing. Knowing how unprepared (when it comes to investing) college graduates and others who enter the work force tend to be, this read reinforces just how needed a book like this is, and how valuable and relevant its content is for the newer investor. It's also valuable for the less-than-successful who are now willing to adopt a more reliable investment approach. Many habits and emotional swings undermine the best intentions and, without a disciplined and simplified strategy to investing, most investors become underperformers, and disillusioned. What this author has accomplished is a pathway that will empower investors to approach their personal finances with a sense of confidence and conviction that will build a lasting foundation in their investments."

Greg Vincenti
Former Senior Vice President/ Branch Manager and Mentor to Wes Rutledge

"This is a great read for parents, grandparents and especially young adults who want to build financial wealth and independence. Wes's years of experience shine through in these pages and remind me of all the great advice he has given me over the years. In his book, he talks about life and how to deal with the times when we might be afraid, overwhelmed or just a little lost. His engaging style just puts you at ease. This book showcases an excellent philosophy for long-term success!"

Jill Joseph Bell
Chief Marketing and Communications Officer

"I expected this book to be beneficial to my two college-aged children, and it is. But what surprised me was how much I learned and will apply in my own future financial decision-making. Wes frames the conversation in a way that's welcoming to anyone who is fairly novice in the investment arena, and his book is sure to be a powerful resource for individuals and organizations alike."

Rena Sharpe
Chief Operating Officer, Goodwill Kentucky

"I really enjoyed reading this book and learned *a lot*. I finally understand that investing shouldn't be a fast horse race but a long-term build, which actually releases a lot of stress. Some of my favorite aspects of the book include how Wes related investing to real-life concepts (e.g., teaching a man to fish). I also enjoyed the italicized questions because there were multiple times I was actually thinking the question before I read it."

Angela Edlin
Young Adult and First-time Investor

"*So Dad, How Can I Make Dollars & Sense?* is a must-read, mind-shifting book for men and women in their 20s and 30s, beginning to grapple with the complexities of managing the earnings of their careers, being smart about unexpected windfalls (like inheritance) and investing for the future."

Kate Colbert
Business Owner, Higher Education Consultant and Author of *Think Like a Marketer: How a Shift in Mindset Can Change Everything for Your Business*

"A practical, enjoyable book that provides an in depth, experienced outlook on a strategic approach to investing — rather than the approach that is often taken nowadays of 'just hope it works itself out.' One of the things that I like most about this book is its consistency. While Wes addresses different concepts in each chapter, he does so in a way that ties it all together and allows the reader to understand not just the basic messages, but also the *why* behind each message. I love Wes's unique approach to the book's topic; he successfully simplifies the concept of investing and having a financial strategy but keeps the conversation light and uses memorable stories to explain each concept."

David W. Johns
Editorial Board Member, Sales Representative (Age 28)

"The 'So Dad' conversations with young adults in this book are realistic and entertaining. The book's humor and stories will keep readers engaged and prevent them from zoning out. Along the way, timely investing philosophies (often explained with eye-catching sayings that makes you remember) are discussed. This is a fun read (as intended), with important learning material sprinkled throughout the book. The book really encourages you to think hard about the concepts explained. The author's real-world experiences are relatable to young readers and help bridge the gap from financial concepts to important life decisions that will last a lifetime."

Andrew Bronger

Vice President – Investments / Wealth Advisor

"As a CPA and a father of a 19-year-old, I consider this book a must-read. Wes explains the world of finances and how to navigate the risk with precision and clarity, which is a gift. Read this book from cover to cover, take copious notes, apply over time, and watch your investment grow. Practice patience.

Peter A. Margaritis, CSP, CPA

Author of *Taking the Numb Out of Numbers: Explaining and Presenting Financial Information with Confidence and Clarity*

"I have known Wes Rutledge for more than 25 years, and respect and trust him enough to have enlisted his professional help and advice in managing my daughter's college fund. His book accurately meets an important and critical need of improving public knowledge of sound financial principles. Reading these pages will earn you a great return on the investment of your time."

Michael L. Seebert

Retired Telecommunications Executive

"I'm all too familiar the 'deer in the headlights' look on the faces of young adults entering the workforce as they are onboarding and making life-changing decisions about financial planning, retirement, and insurance. As a market leader for Engage Mentoring, having spent 12 years in the insurance industry as an employee benefits professional, and a recovering overspender/underbudgeter myself, I have seen first-hand the issues addressed in Wes Rutledge's book. Wes lays a solid foundation for readers, including influencers, addressing our need as mentors to understand the basics of investing and outlining how to have easy conversations to help build trust and wealth for individuals in the field or within the family. Wes's stories and experiences with his kids helped me understand the importance of teaching my daughter 'how to fish' instead of 'feeding' her. I'm sure to go back to this book as a reference for years to come.

Michael Rider

Market Leader, Engage Mentoring, and Owner,
Rider Risk Management Services, LLC

WES RUTLEDGE

So Dad, How Can I Make Dollars & Sense?

Wealth-Building
Insights for When
Adulting Begins
in EARNest

SILVER TREE
PUBLISHING

Editing by:
Kate Colbert

Cover design and typesetting by:
Courtney Hudson

First edition, July 2019

ISBN: 978-1-948238-13-7

Library of Congress Control Number: 2019938170

Created in the United States of America

Dedication

This book is intended for two audiences:

Young adults, and those who love, support and influence them. May the insights shared in the following pages provide you the confidence to truly own your financial futures, the knowledge to grow and succeed on your own terms, and the permission to be your very best selves. Whether you're 23 or 53, your needs, fears, wishes and aspirations are what inspired me to write this book. This is for you.

FOR YOUNG ADULTS

This book is my attempt to help you prepare for the times when your schooling is over, and the financial planning phase of your lives begins.

I've spent a lot of time with college students, and I love being around them. At the time of this book's publication, my oldest daughter is 25 and recently graduated with a college degree in communications, and my 22-year-old son is a senior business student studying marketing. I love talking with their friends, classmates and fraternity brothers, and, aside from it being fun, I genuinely enjoy *working* with them too — watching them learn, develop and begin to really contribute to the world with their talents and skills.

But I've enjoyed it not as just a dad. For many years, I was lucky enough to work with other undergraduate students who served as interns at organizations where I worked and volunteered. Outside my life as a financial consultant, I volunteered with a large civic organization — The KY Derby Festival. The Derby Festival promotes the Louisville community by producing about 70 events each year during the 2-3 weeks leading up to the KY Derby. (Maybe you've heard of that race?) During those weeks, the KY Derby Festival entertains in excess of 1.5 million people and produces an economic impact to the community of more than $125 million. What began with me passing out t-shirts and hanging event banners evolved into greater responsibilities. I progressed all the way up the chain of command and, after nearly 30 years, I eventually served as the Chairman of its Board of Directors. Each year, new interns came in, learned, contributed and moved on. After all those years, I knew I wanted to continue working and helping young people. What they taught me was perhaps even greater than what I taught them.

This book is dedicated to you, and all young people, as you begin your lives "adulting." It's my attempt to share with you some of the advice and wisdom that I've collected along the way. But it's not just college students for whom this book tolls. It's dedicated to young servicemembers who stand up and serve this great country, and veterans just finishing their enlistments and striking out to build civilian futures. This book is for those who study the trades, work in factories and small businesses, and perform the vital services of enduring and emerging industries. It's for the artists, engineers, chefs and restaurant workers, doctors, nurses, dental staff members and hair stylists. As a dad, I want to help you prepare for the time when you sit down with an investment professional. I want to help you develop a sense of what you are trying to accomplish, and help you avoid the feeling that perhaps you're getting ripped off or possibly doing something dumb with your money.

FOR THE INFLUENCERS

The parents and grandparents, professors and instructors, mentors and friends of young adults: This book is intended to be a tool to help you teach and support our next generation. Let my stories and methods supplement the facts and figures you teach. As companies shift away from employer-directed pensions toward employee-guided 401(k) plans and similar retirement plans, our young adults will need to become more financially engaged than ever before. They will need to do more than just contribute to these programs. They will need to actively participate in them. Additionally, in the future, they may also receive residuals from *your* plans and other assets as you pass them along. Becoming more knowledgeable at a younger age will serve them well as they prepare for their futures.

Challenge them to ask questions, debate different approaches, and experience world and market realities. Doing so now will help them progress through their financial futures with fewer stings, bumps and bruises than the world might otherwise bring those who don't have the benefit of your guidance and perspectives. I'm a retired financial consultant and a dedicated dad who wrote a book designed to help the student, the teacher and the institution alike. I hope you find *So Dad, How Can I Make Dollars & Sense?* to be a resource worth sharing, praising and teaching from.

Table of Contents

Foreword

LARRY GOLDSTEIN, PRESIDENT, CAMPUS STRATEGIES, LLC

When I was young, there was no one in my family or our network of friends who understood the investment world. Frankly, we had no resources to invest anyway, so it wasn't something I gave much thought while growing up.

After returning from the service and earning an accounting degree, I began working in public accounting — but on the tax side. Beyond the investment knowledge I needed to properly report client transactions in their tax returns, I knew little to nothing about the world of investments even then. I remained generally ignorant of investing the entire time I worked in public accounting and this continued even after I transitioned into higher education finance.

My first higher education employer, The University of Chicago, offered me the opportunity to establish my initial investment portfolio through contributions of a portion of my earnings that they would match. I took advantage of the program and needed to make only one decision — how much to direct to fixed income investments and how much to invest in equities. Being somewhat unsophisticated about it, I opted for equal distribution. It wasn't the wisest decision at the time, but it didn't end up hurting me too much in the long run because the equities grew significantly, resulting in a more appropriate distribution.

A few years later in my mid-30s, I was approached by a personal financial advisor about investing in mutual funds. Working with that advisor, I made my first investments as a private investor. After a couple job changes with attendant relocations, I formed a relationship with a new advisor with whom I have worked for nearly 20 years now. Together, we have embarked on a course of investing in funds that have performed exceptionally well given my level of risk comfort and overall investment objectives. As I near retirement, I feel my wife and I will have the resources we need to enjoy a comfortable lifestyle.

As you can quickly see, until somewhat later in life, I was never intentional about securing my financial future. As someone who worked with accounting, and then higher education finance, I understood the importance of savings. But that's only one form of investing — and in some ways, the least sophisticated one. Although I devoted significant attention to my employers' investments to ensure proper accounting and reporting, I didn't take an active role with my own portfolio.

After I became the chief financial officer and treasurer at the University of Louisville, I participated as part of a team of people to ensure the university's investments were well managed. All the while, I didn't add anything to the modest private portfolio I'd begun a number of years earlier. I simply relied on the employer-matched program I'd started early in my career, and continued it with each subsequent job.

I now wonder if I'd had access to a publication like this one — especially one so easy to comprehend — whether I would have achieved financial security much earlier in my life. At a minimum, I would have recognized much earlier that the most important aspect of building financial security is active participation in the process. Yes, I've relied on an employer-provided fund to build a good portion of my portfolio. However, I've been self-employed for the past 20 years, so it was important for me to take complete control of that portfolio. My advisor and I meet regularly to review the funds I'm invested in and make changes as needed. I don't study the markets, so I've never approached him to recommend a new investment for my portfolio, but I've considered the pros and cons of each option he's suggested before pulling the trigger.

Using the information provided in Wes Rutledge's remarkable book (which I plan to buy for my children and adult grandchildren), young people can enter the world of investing with the knowledge they will need to make informed choices. As suggested in the dedication, the book is targeted to young adults and people who have their best interests at heart. Wes's conversational writing style will be more comfortable for the former, but the latter should not be put off by the examples targeted to that younger generation. These young folks need to be reached in a way that is appealing to them so they will not shy away from the important messages contained in each chapter.

This book is a gift (or investment) that will keep on giving (or providing a return). I had the honor of reading two preliminary drafts of the book and it gets better each time. I'm not at the stage in my life when I likely will read the final version again. But I'll bet the young people who embrace it will come back to it time and time again for insights to help guide them as their financial resources and needs change throughout their lives. Some of the best messages in the book will take on new significance as the years go by.

Congratulations to you, readers, for wisely picking up this book, and for using it to advance you toward your vision of financial security!

LARRY GOLDSTEIN
President, Campus Strategies, LLC
Author of *College and University Budgeting: A Guide for Academics and Other Stakeholders, 5th Edition*

Introduction

First things first. Thank you for picking up this book and spending some time with it! With countless books, papers, articles and blogs written on every subject under the stars, the fact that you are looking at these words right this moment deserves my deep appreciation. I'm grateful for your attention. No matter how this book has made it into your hands, please know that I'm thankful and honored for each minute you spend absorbing its ideas and considering my thoughts.

That said, let's start with **"Why another business book?"** Sure, I know there are thousands of business books. But given my experiences with family wealth and working with young people, I wanted to do my part to foster a better starting position (or hand-off, so to speak) between the parents and influencers of young adults and the financial professionals who will ultimately serve them. I wanted to build a tool to help spark conversations, inspire thoughts, and focus attention — as it pertains to money, savings and investing — in the areas where schools, institutions and many households tend to come up perhaps a little short.

So, to introduce this book to you, and perhaps save some of you a little time, let me begin with what this book *isn't*. This really isn't a "what is" book. Sure, it has some terms and definitions, but it isn't really about "what is a stock? What is a bond? What is a mutual fund or any other product?"

It isn't a "rule book." It doesn't go over retirement distribution requirements, or potential tax saving strategies. It isn't a "how to pick a hot stock" guidebook. This book won't tell you what to do. It won't tell you what *not* to do. "OK, well great," you might be thinking. "What does this book do? — And, for brevity, what *specifically* does it do?"

A CONVERSATION YOU'VE BEEN WAITING FOR

This book is a conversational approach to help young adults and first-time investors prepare to sit down with investment professionals the first few times. It should help you understand what you really are trying to do, what to expect and how you might want to operate. The book is presented as a conversation between me and my kids (*"So Dad ..."*), and I'm confident you'll see yourself in the smart questions they ask me throughout. By listening in, so to speak, to this conversation, you'll learn much.

Specifically:

- *Chapter 1* will help you focus on your purpose. Why are you investing versus saving? This chapter deeply explores how trust, risk and learning need to fit within the relationship between the young adult and the financial pro.

- *Chapter 2* is about direction and planning. For many, the term "investing" is like the word "vacation." When we gather together with our family and friends to talk about going on "vacation" this year, that's just the subject of the conversation — not the actual destination or the means to get there. "Investing" is similar. It's the subject. But after determining that we want to go on "vacation," we must still decide on a destination, plan a route, figure out a budget and then start packing before we head out the door. Likewise, when we decide to "invest," we really should think about where we want to end up, plan a route and a budget, and then start packing.

- *Chapter 3* will help you appreciate the psychology of investing. It aims to help you understand that we might need some rules and policies to guide us when our emotions could get the better of us.

- *Chapter 4* begins the deep dive into how we start designing and constructing our wealth, as opposed to "just sticking some money in there and hoping it goes up."

- *Chapter 5* has us break down our situations and address our biggest fears — the fears of potentially doing something dumb with our money or getting ripped off by someone (or something) else. This tough little chapter gives us some great weapons to experiment with — math and time.

- *Chapter 6* pivots the conversation. We begin shifting the focus from my answers to your investment questions, to *your* answers to your investment questions.

- *Chapter 7* helps you expand your answers to even further lengths. That's right ... we focus on your answers; your choices and your preferences.

- *Chapter 8* wraps things up with freedom. It helps us move from the science of investing to the art of investing and gives you the encouragement and confidence you'll need as you head into the human resources (HR) or financial professional's office.

So, in essence, I'm going to take you on a journey through the up and down markets I saw in my career — from historical stock market crash lows to market conditions that had stocks exploding in value right before your eyes … only to watch it happen again in a different way. And, I'll tell you how we handled it, and not only survived — we thrived.

"Wait! This isn't a history book is it?" No, not by design, but I do want you to understand the old adage "History repeats itself" can be very true. The world and the economy are changing and getting faster — but many of the underlying reasons are all the same. Perhaps its fear affecting our actions — or greed, or power. They have in the past, and I'm confident each of them will pop back up in the future (in some fashion). My goal, with this book is to help you handle them when they do.

OK, but why you and why now? Because it's up to you! The person in charge of taking care of your financial future isn't your employer with their pensions, like it once was. It isn't the federal government with Social Security — even like it might seem today. It's up to you, and the time is now, because every day that you embrace learning and working with this subject increases the probability that you'll do smarter and wiser things to take care of yourself. (That's one of those spiffy lessons we talk about in chapter 5.) And smarter and wiser are two great components of success. I hope this book will help you just like my own young adults Make Dollars and Sense.™

Enjoy!

CHAPTER 1

Yeah!!! I finally landed my first REAL job, but before I could get the first check home, the HR people wanted me to think about putting money into the company retirement plan. Wuwt??

WOOHOO!!! Grandpa John named me in his will and left me $50,000. Now what do I do?

My parents keep telling me there won't be any Social Security or Medicare insurance when I get to be their age, so how am I going to have enough to retire and take care of myself and take great vacations?

How do I avoid getting ripped off or sold stuff I won't want or need in the future?

How do I know the "professional" isn't just after my money? Does he or she care about me - at least a little?

So Dad, how can I be smarter with my money? How can I make dollars and sense?

"Teachers open the door. You enter by yourself."

– Chinese Proverb

The day finally snuck up on me. My kids started focusing on money — and not just spending it. OK, they're 25 and 22 years old and aren't "kids" anymore. But who'd have any idea what I was talking about if I wrote "my young adults" or wouldn't crack up if I referred to them as "my fully grown offspring" or "my favorite young professionals?" My daughter was being encouraged to start contributing to a 401(k) at her job, and my son was starting his final year in business school, a place where you can't help but learn and wonder about money.

These initial conversations about money management were much easier for me than for them. It's a path I had been down many, many times over my 27-year career as a financial consultant. But for them — even though they had grown up with a financial professional at their beck and call — it was the first time they were directly facing major financial questions. Sure, they had mastered the "Dad, can you spare $20 for gas?" question long ago, but this time it was different. They each came in to get some advice and help instead of money. But I should state it correctly. They came to me, so I could tell them what to do. *"Cut to the chase, Dad, what am I supposed to do?"*

Building wealth. Protecting wealth. Using wealth. Transferring wealth. Start the cycle again! I faced these issues thousands of times throughout the years with my clients. It's the financial cycle of life. And now I'm starting it all over again with my kids, their friends and other young adults. Up until now, my most memorable advice to young adults might have been "Don't drink anything blue" (which I've said many times). Now, my advice centers on thinking and learning a little about **invest-ments** — before you sit down with a professional, because in the very near future, most of you will have to address similar finan-cial questions.

 Investments: Financial products of various types (also known as securities)

Maybe it's because you have started a new job and you're sitting with a human resources (HR) professional, being asked whether you want to participate in the company's retirement plan (and how much you want to contribute, and to which funds!). Some of you might be in the very enviable position where your income is greater than your "out-go" (i.e., your regular expenses) and you don't want to let all that extra money slip away or possibly make a mistake with it. Some of you reading this book might be given money or investments by a relative, either as a gift or an inheritance. Suddenly, you're faced with the question: Where do you begin when working with money?

Your parents and grandparents might very well be the people you turn to for advice, or they might refer you to a financial profes-sional. For some, going to a financial pro might seem like going to a restaurant in a foreign land. You need to stand at the counter and attempt to choose something off a menu you can't read, and the server speaks in a fast and different language. Good luck with that first bite!

Of course, I could have told my kids what to do. In these instances, I knew them very well — better than they knew themselves with this subject. But this is where an ancient proverb hits the nail squarely on the head. Lao Tzu said "Give a man a fish and you feed him for a day. Teach him how to fish and you feed him for a lifetime." If I wanted to cut right to the chase, I could customize the answers, and tell my kids exactly what to do. I could give them a great big, freakin' delicious fish!

But if I did, they would always be reliant on me or someone else to give or sell them fish. And some day, some crafty lobster salesman might convince them that lobsters are just like fish, but better. Then the octopus salesman might slide in and say, "If you like fish and lobster, then you should try this little eight-legged piece of seafood! Because that's what they all are, right? Seafood." And there you go thinking an octopus is just the same as a fish. Oh, boy.

Instead, if I taught my adult children what a fish is and how to catch fish, they still might want to eat a lobster or an octopus, but they wouldn't have been misled into thinking it was the same thing as a fish. If I've taught them well, my kids could chose not to fish and only buy fish for the rest of their lives. And that would be OK too, because with their solid knowledge about fish and fishing, they won't be as apt to make common fish mistakes, or get sold fish they didn't want or need. And they could live happy fish-filled lives.

The same is true with investments. If my kids learn what investments are and why they might want to consider them, they'll have a much better chance of successfully investing money, avoiding some common mistakes and neither feeling like they're getting ripped off or sold stuff they don't want or need. That same advice is true for you.

Maybe your parents or grandparents have invested successfully and can just tell you what to do. Hopefully they'll teach you how and why to invest — because most probably, they won't always be there to tell you what to do (or do it for you) for the rest of your life. And in this very realistic scenario of eventually being on your own, the investment questions pivot to: "Where do you begin?" and "Who do you trust, and why?"

So, in my kids' instances, I gave them a fish and told them their immediate investment answers, based on my experience and expertise. But I also told them it was time for them to learn how to fish (invest) a little — which also meant that they would need to know why, as well. *"Please, please, please, Dad can't you boil this down? Cut to the chase and tell me what I really need to know! I don't have 27 years to learn this stuff for myself."*

If my kids learn what investments are and why they might want to consider them, they'll have a much better chance of successfully investing money, avoiding some common mistakes and neither feeling like they're getting ripped off or sold stuff they don't want or need. That same advice is true for you.

OK, OK, I'll tell you the basic info in this easy-to-read book. But you're right — it is about learning. I'll tell you what I think will help you, and why I think it's important. I'll tell how I came to learn it myself, and how it was tested under the best investing conditions and the worst times, too. Hopefully, after reading this book you'll have the tools you need to start talking about investing ... and it surely won't take 27 years (or 27 months, or 27 weeks, or even 27 days) for you to get through it.

Then you should have some idea of what you are trying to accomplish when you sit down with a financial professional. You and the pro will select plans and methods that fit you best and that fall within their realms of experience and expertise. You will enter the proverbial fish market looking for fish, or head to the octopus shop because you're looking for an octopus. And you'll know the difference between them.

"WHERE DO YOU BEGIN?" AND "WHO DO YOU TRUST, AND WHY?"

These are not easy questions. I remember distinctly grappling with them myself when I was about my daughter's age (and maybe yours) when I first began my career — and I was on the other side of the table!! I was 25 years old, hired as the professional and in for the ride of a lifetime.

Growing up, I could never have imagined not having a dependable salary or a predictable income. Yet, as career events unfolded, I took a job where my compensation was 100% commission-based. And I took that job just three and a half months before the worst financial market correction in history. How's that for timing?! While my initial training and licensing prepared me to begin a career as what was called a "registered representative" (rep, for short) for a **securities firm**, truth be told, I was hired for **commissioned sales.** I was taught to **cold-call** individuals and businesses, attempting to build relationships that would result in a commissionable transaction — either by helping the client to buy

 Securities Firm: A company that buys, sells and manages investments for clientele.

Commission Sales: No salary or fee. Compensation is determined by a % of sales.

Cold-Call: An unsolicited call to an unknown potential client, also known as a prospect.

a security to add to their holdings, or sell one that they had previously purchased because now it wasn't performing as hoped (or it no longer fit their needs). If I was lucky, maybe do both!

While I was hired as a salesperson initially, that was not my end game. I had entered the securities world to learn the business and take over my father's practice. After more than 40 years in the industry, he was preparing to retire, and I was to be the next wave of expertise. Six months of cold-calling went by with very spotty results, at best. I merged my few clients into my dad's practice and started learning how to be a true consultant.

At first, I had a set of pretty simple questions about my dad's practice: "Why do people come to him?" And "Why do people invest?" These questions were vastly different from those of my training class peers. Most of them were grappling with who they should call as potential clients and how to qualify them. How should they start the conversation, make an appointment, and make a sale/commission? Did they start with questions about the prospect's needs, or just jump in with a product and keep adjusting to whatever response the prospect gave until they either made the sale or were hung up on? This was how we were trained, and the system we were operating under forced most reps to focus on commissions and making money. I was focusing on how to help the clients with their needs.

On October 19, 1987 (now known as Black Monday), the **Dow Jones Industrial Average** (DJIA) dropped 22.6% and lost more than $500 billion in value, a record that today still stands as the largest percentage drop in financial market history.

 Dow Jones Industrial Average: A fixed collection of companies thought to generally represent the industrial aspects of the United States.

The crash in 1987 was a large spectacle in the world. For my grand-parents' generation, it brought back memories (and huge fears) of the 1929 market crash and the Great Depression, which overtook the US in the 1930s. My parents' generation had heard the stories and seen the pictures of the Depression days. Fear and caution were thrust upon them as newspapers, TV and radio re-counted those same stories. My generation (and that of your parents) seemed most concerned with the question of "What does this really mean?" Confusion and caution were the most prevalent emotions.

Market confidence was completely obliterated, and panic among investors was not just in New York or on television; it was in our offices and on our streets. The government had put measures in place to ensure that there wouldn't be a **"run" on the banks** and securities firms, like what had happened in 1929. I remember sitting in the training room when the company's leaders came in to host a firm-wide conference call

 Bank Run: After the crash in 1929, banks were swarmed by customers demanding their deposits be returned to them. They feared the bank would fail and run out of money, and their savings would be lost.

and tell us that we would survive as a business. We were told that we should contact our clients to reassure them. But I didn't have any clients yet, so my job was to make cold-calls.

The very first task of a cold-call to an unknown prospect is to estab-lish trust. After that, we build upon that trust to affect a decision and then initiate an action that results in commissionable transactions. Trust: What a slippery and difficult term to verbalize and describe!

In 1987, the rules for phone sales were much different than they are today. Sales calls to a home happened every hour of every day.

 Financial Markets: Central places where securities are traded.

Caller ID hadn't made it into most homes yet, and if the phone rang, people either answered it or let it go to the answering machine (Yes, there was a separate machine for that function!) in fear that it might be a sales call. New reps would gather a list of what they hoped were qualified prospects and dial away. The goal was to make 20 calls a day. But, right off the bat, I had two strikes against me. Strike one: I was calling with what was essentially a sales call. Strike two: I represented a securities firm, and the **financial markets** were all over the place. While some prospects were scrambling, most were paralyzed with fear. I remember asking myself, "How do I build a whiff of trust in the first few seconds of the call?" Isn't this ironic? Your question, as the client, is who should you trust? And mine, as the professional, was how do I get you to trust me? To be successful and avoid problems, you'll need to be on the same page with your investment professional.

Most of my training class peers were not having great success. At the end of the first year, about two-thirds of them had left the firm, and many had left the industry. To be clear, being a 25-year-old trainee was not the norm. Most trainees were older than me by an average of five years. Some trainees came from the banking industry, looking for freedom and the ability to make more money. Some came from other industries, looking for a faster pace. Nearly all had more business experience than I did, but I had an ace that they didn't. I had begun building a system to help me develop trust and give me the time to survive and let that trust grow — both with the clients and within myself. That's what all the questions at the beginning of this chapter were really about, weren't they — trust?

The most important reason that my dad's clients came to him were because they trusted him. I needed them to trust me, so I worked to become an extension of him. My approach was, "They trusted him — he trusted me — you can trust me." They trusted him because he had proven, often over many years, to be honest and to work hard for their best interests. But being honest and hardworking weren't the only reasons they came and stayed with him. His advice and skills were such that they were happy and satisfied with the performance of their securities and how they were affecting their lives. That's why they came and stayed. I wanted to learn why clients invest in the first place. Take note: You might be asking yourself this very question when you sit down with your first set of retirement forms.

In the very early months of my career that followed, I learned to identify several types of investors. I worked hard to understand why they would invest — you might see yourself in one of these groups.

 One group I called "semi-conscious." That is, they were present at the meeting but not actually engaged in the discussion. Someone referred them to me, and because of that person's stature in their life, they were following through — they felt obligated. Maybe their grandparents wanted to help them start a house fund or supplemental retirement program. Or maybe their parents wanted to help them begin their investing education by giving them money. Surprisingly, some spouses brought their partners so that they would have a face and name "in case something happened" — what I called "the insurance theory." Some would obligingly attend the retirement planning meeting because their employer set up the appointment, established a matching proportion and highly encouraged them to take part in the plan. *The teacher would open the door, hoping the student would enter.*

- Another group I called "conscious but a little short." They knew that they wanted to invest, and quite often had a grand goal in mind, but they were not properly focused. "Vaguely focused" might be a better term. Some of them had been left an inheritance from a parent or grandparent, and they wanted to be good stewards of their gifts. Some were actively trying to save for their retirement or the college education they wanted for their children. Some wanted to do something with their excess earnings but were not sure what it might be. *The student had entered the room but wasn't truly sure of why they were there.*

- A small group I called the "savvy investors" came because they knew what they were doing and had shopped for fair pricing. Typically, they were financially well-educated and liked the level of attention and other services we had to offer. These students entered the room, liked the class and knew what to do. *The teacher could only try to open another door for them.*

- The last group were "the determined ones," and they seemed quite focused. They were there to WIN! They heard that the markets were soaring, and they wanted to be at that party! Maybe their friend or relative had an outstanding opportunity or result, and they wanted to capitalize on or mirror that performance. Some saw opportunities to "Buy Low" when the markets or a specific security fell, with the hopes to "Sell High" and make quick "mega-money." They were sucked into the emotions of the markets, and though they thought they were sound investors, they were applying various gambling tactics for a short-term win. *These students entered the room thinking that they could get an easy A and then head to the next class*

elsewhere. Sometimes they were correct; most often they were surprised at least a little.

As you can see from these different groups, there might have been many different answers to this question of why people invest. But there were many more times when the prospect wasn't sure at all what the answer was — they had no idea why they were doing what they were doing. *I came to believe early in my career that the true reason most of my clients came to invest was to get a better rate of return than the bank was willing to guarantee them (given a certain level of risk) over a defined period.*

I want to be perfectly clear right here. This is not an "anti-bank" statement. To the contrary. Banks and bank safety standards are such that they are some of the most trusted places to store and build wealth. In 1934, because of the 1929 crash, the federal government enacted regulations to strengthen the banks' roles for public financial safety. Banks were not the problem. They were just the competition.

Both my dad's and my goals were to help our clients get better returns than the bank would guarantee with their savings accounts, **Certificates of Deposit** (CDs) and other proprietary products. Understanding this will help shed light on

 Certificate of Deposit (CD): A bank-guaranteed product that promises to pay the holder a specific rate of interest over a specific period and then return the original amount invested back to the holder on a set date.

the process I used to help my clients build wealth. In all my years working in the financial services industry, I never acted as the decision maker for any of my clients' accounts. My clients made their own decisions themselves and bore the risks associated with them. I served as an advisor. While it would have been much easier to operate with discretion (formally granted, written permission) on their behalf, I felt it best for them to understand how they were building their wealth. (And once again, the fish analogy pops to mind.) That's the goal of this book ... to help you learn to start taking control of your investment questions — even if you don't know what they are just yet.

Teachers open the door. You enter by yourself.

TRUST AND RISK – OH, HOW THEY CAN DANCE TOGETHER AND APART!

"So Dad, what do you mean by this?" OK, Let's back up and let me set this up for you. A couple years before I was hired by the securities firm, the Dow Jones Average (DJIA) finally rose above the 1,500 level in December 1985. At the time, this seemed remarkable, because it had taken nearly 10 years for the average to close above the 1,050 mark it established in January 1973. So, to have increased 50% was eyepopping at that time. Even more remarkably, in the next 18 months, the DJIA increased substantially more to close above 2,700 in August 1987. And so, if you're keeping score at home, the DJIA had increased 170% (from 1,000 to 2,700) in less than three years, after being essentially flat for 10 years before. Talk about growth! Think about a tree outside your window or on the corner becoming nearly three times larger than it is right now — in just 3 years. That's some serious shade!

As luck would have it, I was hired just before then in July 1987. Earlier I stated: "Trust: What a slippery and difficult term to verbalize and describe!" Almost immediately, I had to address many questions of trust. Did the clients and prospects trust me as a 25-year-old professional? Would they trust me with their money? Some of it? Most of it? With $5,000? With $50,000? All of it? How much trust did they have? If trust was slippery, risks could have surely accelerated and/or extended the slide.

On October 19, 1987, after sliding downward the past two months, the Dow Jones Average (DJIA) closed nearly 1,000 points lower, at 1,738.74. It fell 508 points that day alone! In less than two months, it lost more than 35% of its value. (What?? Somebody just lopped off a huge hunk of that big old tree?) I had been there for just about four months, and my first days out of the training department were the last days of October. How could I build anyone's trust during such a market downturn? It was easy to trust when everything seemed to have been moving up, but would you trust me when the markets were falling? Would you trust me when you didn't really know what was going on?

It was easy to trust when everything seemed to have been moving up, but would you trust me when the markets were falling? Would you trust me when you didn't really know what was going on?

In late November 1987, while I was still trying to develop my practice, I sheepishly adjusted my sales call approach to one of fact finding. I wanted to build some trust. I called my prospects and asked them if I could get their responses to a few questions. This was NOT a sales call — just information gathering. Once they felt there wasn't much of a risk, many of them were more than willing to extend me a little bit of trust and help me complete some market research.

My questions centered on whether they considered themselves investors. I was trying to determine whether they had money to invest and how much financial knowledge and experience they might have. I used all

 Mutual Fund: A collection of investments that are professionally managed for a specific purpose and are publicly traded within a financial market.

kinds of jargon. As investors, what types of investments did they prefer? Stocks? Bonds? **Mutual Funds?** Money Market accounts? CDs? (Look at me, speaking in a foreign language at the financial food counter.) Gathering this information, I started getting a sense that the people who were most upset were afraid of the risk of losing more money than they already had. I felt so smart asking all these financial questions.

Probing a little deeper, I then asked even more jargon-laced questions. If they had stocks or stock mutual funds, what types did they have? Blue chips? Small caps? Emerging technologies? Did they have any foreign investments? If they had CDs, how long were their maturities? What interest rates were they getting on them? What did their money market account pay? (Do you want some financial fries with your order?) I focused all my small talk on the client's holdings and feelings as they related to the financial industry. But I noticed that the more I recognized their fears as legitimate, the more they told me about those fears. Man, was I smart!

But, let's get this straight — I had been hired, trained and tried to operate on my own. All this talking was great, but I wasn't opening accounts, affecting transactions or making commissions. Smart me — I was failing! In April 1988, I merged my flimsy little practice into my dad's practice to survive. It was either that or start another career elsewhere as many of my training class peers had done.

Watching my dad work with his clients and people that were referred to him, I noticed how different his approach was from mine. While I asked questions about investments, he talked about fears and goals. He was matching their expectations with how much risk they said they could tolerate and looking to increase the returns relative to their responses. He wasn't trying to get a return that was better than the market. He was trying to get a return that was better than the bank would guarantee. The question was not how much they trusted him. The question was how much risk was tolerable to get a better rate of return?

Watching my dad work with his clients and people that were referred to him, I noticed how different his approach was from mine. While I asked questions about investments, he talked about fears and goals.

Risk is a strange thing. When faced with risk, many people use emotion instead of logic to grapple with their fears. Risk seems small and slim when things are going well, but in the blink of an eye, it can grow to an immense and overpowering giant. Or does it?

Think for a minute about the last horror film you watched or an old episode of a Scooby-Doo cartoon. Everything was going along just fine until they walked up to the door of that house. What's the risk of going to the door? Very slim, right? And what's the risk of peeking in when the door just mysteriously creeps open? They're just curious, right? What's the risk in that? Then they look over to the corner and there's a dead body lying on the floor. Holy crap! BIG RISK! BIG EMOTION: FEAR! RUN!

But logically, wasn't there ample risk when they took that first step toward the door? Had the risk changed at all? Nope. The crime and danger were already there. The difference was they suddenly became aware of the risk, and their fear grew suddenly. So suddenly, in fact, that now a sudden response was needed. Or was it? When Shaggy and Scooby were hiding in the barrel, weren't Velma, Daphne and Freddy looking for clues to solve the mystery?

On the other side, when things can't seem to get any better, happiness and contentment fill the air. Who thinks about risks then? The truth is that every day the markets go up, so does the risk — and most people don't notice. Many people are so lost in their blissful, happy state of making money or "being right" with their investment decisions that they fail to recognize that their risk is growing. Things are worth more, so there is more at risk. Ironically, when the markets are falling, risk suddenly comes into focus and can look much larger ... and trust can slip away (sometimes with astonishing speed). Learning to understand and master the dance between trust and risk was the first lesson I needed to learn. ***Teachers open the door.***

The truth is that every day the markets go up, so does the risk — and most people don't notice. Many people are so lost in their blissful, happy state of making money or "being right" with their investment decisions that they fail to recognize that their risk is growing.

In my early days, having conversations about risk with clients tended to raise their fears instead of lowering them, and again more jargon didn't help. **Market risks, interest rate risks, political or**

government risks, credit risks, inflation risks, currency risks, and many others would feel like a pile of bricks on their chests. (Doesn't that text block to the right seem heavy?)

The more we talked about those risks, the greater their fears would rise, and their trust would fall. Such conversations almost always tended to paralyze my clients with fear. When talking about how much risk you could tolerate — particularly after the 1987 market crash — clients generally answered, "Not very much at all, if any." How could I build trust when the fear of risk was so great? *I had to enter by myself.*

About six months into my business partnership with my dad, I very distinctly

 Market Risks: The risk that the entire market would decline.

Interest Rate Risks: The risk that the interest rates would increase, making current products less valuable.

Political Risks: The risk that the foreign governments would act in ways to de-value their own country's investment products.

Credit Risks: The risk that the companies or government agencies could act in ways to hurt their ability to repay their debts.

Inflation Risks: The risk that prices of goods and services would increase.

Currency Risks: The risk that the exchange rates of currency between countries changes to negatively affect the current holder.

remember asking him why he never really marketed or sold many **shares** of stock of corporations other than **utilities** at that time. He said people were afraid of the markets, and it was easier to help them

Shares/Stocks:
Transferrable units of
ownership in a company.
For this book, generally
traded publicly at
various markets.

Utility(ies): A company that
provides a community with
electricity, natural gas, water
or sewerage services.

Bond: A debt, issued
by a corporation or
government entity, that
paid interest and was to
be re-paid to the owner
at a specific date in the
future. Think of a corporate
or government IOU
with interest.

get a better rate of return
with a **bond** (and its limited
guarantees) than risk money
with stocks, which carried
no guarantees — even if
there might be substantially
more potential return with
some stocks. (Is it wiser to
not walk toward that creepy
old house at all?)

With this in mind, I felt
I could build trust if I could
calm clients' fears and ease
their emotions. But to do
so, I had to stop talking
about stocks, bonds and
all types of financial jargon
altogether, and just talked to
them about being afraid.

The question I used most
to help them learn to deal
with their fears was "What's the safest way to cross an extremely busy
street?" Of course, my question triggered all sorts of questions from
the client: "What did this have to do with investing? Which street?
At what time of day? What did I mean by busy?" Just like my survey
questions, these questions started a dialog through which I could
start building trust.

By far, the most common answer to my question of how to cross the
street was to "look both ways and proceed with caution." "Surely,
you're kidding!" was my frequent response. I then talked about going

to the corner, following the stop light signals, and waiting for the sign to change to WALK. I then asked about people who ran the stop lights, or a possible drunk driver.

We then talked about other methods to cross the street. Police escort? Pole vault? Tunnel under? We talked of other risks: Could we be hurt landing from the pole vault (assuming we knew how to do it and had a pole)? What if there was an earthquake? Our scenarios kept going further and further out, and then I would lead them to my own deduced answer. (Kinda like I'm doing with you now, right?)

The safest way I could think to cross the street was in an armored tank. Of course, we knew this was a quite expensive method. It certainly wouldn't get us there quickly, particularly if we had to order one and have it delivered. Then we would need a place to store it and someone to drive it or teach us how to drive it ourselves. Carried to this level, our fears had grown so far out of proportion that we had "hunkered down" in a tank mentality toward crossing the street. But the clients knew that a tank wasn't really necessary to cross a street.

Most investors hadn't experienced the same performance that the markets had. Their homes hadn't lost value. They still had CDs, savings and money market accounts that were unaffected.

As I had discovered earlier, most were afraid of future losses, even though they had not personally lost anything close to the level of decline that the markets had. So, it wasn't necessary to hunker down simply because the markets went down.

With this exercise, we were addressing their fears with logic and building the trust necessary to begin talking about making investments. (We were solving this mystery!) I had moved into matching their expectations with their tolerance for risk and looked to increase the return relative to their responses. The doors had been opened, and we were entering together.

? **Something to Ponder After Chapter 1:** When it comes to your money and your future, how important are trust, a sense of purpose and communication to you?

Dollars and Sense

Young Adults:

"Where to begin?" This is generally the first question that comes rolling out when we start thinking about what to do as we begin making real money. In most instances, you're going to be asked to consider spending money in certain ways before you get that first check home. "Do you want to participate in the company retirement plan?" "Do you want health or life insurance?"

Typically, we pass these questions to someone we trust — with the hope that we don't do something "dumb" and either waste the money or get ripped off by some other slick person. We might turn to our parents, grandparents, neighbor, employer or friends because they are more knowledgeable or have some wisdom. But what if they aren't experienced or have only bad experiences to share?

"Where to begin?" That's what this first chapter has been all about. It centers around developing trust, understanding risk and becoming more knowledgeable. It has us consider why we are investing, and leads us to the next step: How do we want to do it? And that's really the purpose of this whole book — helping you identify what you want to do, how you want to do it and why. The fear of wasting money, the fear of getting ripped off, the fear of risk(s), the fear of the unknown — how do we address all these fears? The answer lies in learning and developing a special trust in professionals. **It's where we begin.**

Influencers:

This first chapter has been dedicated to trust, risk and learning. These issues are as old as time itself. We're told that Eve was coerced into trusting the snake and then used Adam's trust in her to pull him in, as well. Did they know the risks? Talk about getting ripped off!! And then the real learning began!

Parents and grandparents protect their children by teaching them early. As they grow, that trust is extended to their teachers and leaders. And when the children are old enough, they venture out into the world. Their first tasks are to figure out what to do — and who to trust. They'll draw upon what they've learned and the advice you gave them. Hopefully, that advice contained two little phrases: Keep Learning and Trust Carefully.

Teachers open the door. You enter by yourself.

And yes, I did mingle an ancient proverb, a teaching of Lao Tzu and Scooby-Doo (and now the images of Adam and Eve, too) in this lesson. When teaching, we use what might work, right?

CHAPTER 2

Remember the first time you drove the car by yourself? Was it a quick trip up to the store? Could it have been cruising over to your friend's house? Maybe it was heading to the movie theater or mall? Even if you had been to all these places before, now that you were totally in control of the car by yourself, were you heightened to the question, "How do I get there?"

Does the Google Maps app spell out the route to your "Spring Break" or "Weekend Away" trips?

Isn't there a path of study to your chosen degree, trade or military career?

Aren't directions and plans necessary to get you where you want to go?

"You've got to be very careful if you don't know where you are going, because you might not get there."

– Yogi Berra

OK, you're sitting in the HR office and they've asked if you want to participate in the company retirement plan. *"So Dad, retirement? That's 30 or 40 years from now — when I'm old. What do they mean participate — start sticking money in and saving it?"* In the simplest form, yes. Yes, you could save for retirement with guaranteed returns. But the retirement account is much more than a savings account. It allows you to make investments — to potentially get a better rate of return than the stated, guaranteed rate (the trusted rate, so to speak). *"Are you going to go through that trust and risk thing again, Dad?"* No, but you're beginning to think along the right lines. With more risk, there may be the potential for more return. *"But, more risk of loss, too, right?"* Correct! — You were paying attention. But, let's not start hunkering down in our conversation right now. How about we think about trying to build your retirement account instead of just saving for it?

"Build it? Are you nuts? I don't know where to begin trying to build it." Well, you wouldn't just go to Home Depot, buy some wood and start tossing up a house, would you? You'd have to think about it a little — figure out how you want to live, set some priorities and start scratching out some details to start building it. Building a retirement account works very similarly. Building personal wealth works the same way, too. Sure, you can just put your money in a retirement account and hope things work out. You can also just buy lottery tickets and hope you win. But Yogi is right. "You've got to be very careful if you don't know where you are going, because you might

not get there." *"But I don't know where or how to start."* I know.
It's OK, I've been there many times. I had to figure it out early in my
career too.

For the first six months of my partnership with my dad, I fielded
questions, researched ideas, made presentations, learned more
about trading institutionally and earned a few commissions. But
mostly, I continued to build upon what I had learned about trust
and risk. I was beginning to think that I knew why the clients were
investing with us, but all of them were so very different. What was
their common denominator? The more I struggled with this question,
the more I felt like I was floundering. I couldn't figure out where I was
going. I could take orders and answer questions, but I wasn't really
advising or guiding the clients. *There I was again — back at the fast
food counter in a foreign land.* How could I be better at helping them?

The rebound from the crash
of Black Monday took a little
time. The markets produced just
enough up and down movements
to keep everyone on their toes.
Fear wasn't quick to subside

 Maturities: The
stated length of time
a CD, bond or other
debt security will last.

but, by March 1988, the DJIA had risen back above 2,000. While
this was more than 700 points below its highest peak, it was solidly
higher than the crash lows. Our business was still moving forward
on a mostly bond and utility stock platform. We were succeeding
because we could find bonds with higher rates, longer **maturities**,
and superior credit ratings than the banks were offering on their CDs
and money market accounts.

At the end of April 1988, my dad made the announcement to the firm
that he was going to retire at the end of the year. The practice was to
become mine solely, and I needed to figure out how to make it my

own and build upon it. *"What?! The new dude speaking in a language I don't understand is going to be the head of the store?"* I was just short of my 26th birthday. At this point in time, I had figured out why clients had come to my dad, but I wasn't yet sure why they would work with me.

One of the first things taught in sales training was that, to be effective, the seller must believe in the product and then transfer that belief to the prospect. That was true for every transaction. To sell a bond, the rep had to help the client believe the project was worthwhile, the terms of the instrument were fair, and the probability of repayment was high. So, that was how I approached bond sales. But I felt there was more to the transaction than just that. I was responsible for the product. Safety and interest rates were just part of the factors I should look at with clients. These were my tools to build trust and help clients get a better rate of return. This is what I believed. But to help the clients best, I needed to understand what they believed. The casual conversations about risk and fears needed to change, and so did my questions — but in which direction?

To help the clients best, I needed to understand what they believed.

To help you best, the financial pro will need to know what you believe — and the other way around, too. You should know what they believe. That tingle you might have just felt was the concept of trust growing within you a little. It's one thing to trust the professional's knowledge, but are they wise? Do they care how you feel? *"So Dad, I might not even know how I feel. Today, I might not have any feeling. Or I might be nervous, scared, aggressive, in love — whatever."*

You're right. Does your financial advisor recognize your feelings, or
do they just plod on through with their agendas?

My quest to understand what
my clients believed and the
search for the common denominator didn't start very well.
Once again, my simple and
direct questions produced more
questions about what I was
asking than any solid responses.

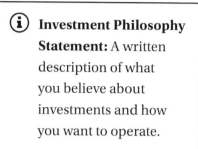

**(i) Investment Philosophy
Statement:** A written
description of what
you believe about
investments and how
you want to operate.

The only thing I could figure out was that they couldn't tell me very
well what they wanted or believed. *Sound familiar?* To help them,
I needed to tell them what I believed and see if they agreed with
me or had different ideas. I had to build and share my **investment
philosophy statement** and see where they agreed or differed. This
was my guide to advising my clients — my map, so to speak. The
common denominator was me. But to understand it better, I need to
explain how it came to be.

WOULD YOU RATHER SHOP OR SURF TODAY?

There were several components that I took into consideration when
crafting my investment philosophy statement. I looked at my first
question about why people invest, and the investments that my
dad's clients had held, to analyze their successes and identify trends.
Many of the securities had been in place for long periods of time and
were performing well. There was much to learn from so much data.

The process of creating my statement started with my general
approach toward risk. While I am not a fanatic about winning at

all cost, I don't like to lose at much of anything — especially as it pertains to money. I focused tightly on not losing money. I viewed risk much the same way my clients did. The market jitters and the client fears had me hunkering down right along with them. I was afraid that if they lost money, I would lose them as clients. After all, who would want to invest with a professional who loses money for their clients? So, to limit the potential for loss, I started by addressing risk logically and focused on *probabilities* instead of just looking at the possibilities the investments might possess. What was most likely to happen?

While I am not a fanatic about winning at all cost, I don't like to lose at much of anything — especially as it pertains to money.

At the core of my investment philosophy statement (what I truly believe and how I operate) is this: I am a value-oriented investor. It is the first, and most important, tenet to my statement. To the rest of the world outside the finance industry, I would be called a shopper. Maybe my philosophy was shaped by my upbringing, or maybe it was molded by the environment in which I started my career, but I first approached investments from a value perspective. From this perspective, there are only three levels at which a security could trade:

1. At fair value

2. At a discount-to-fair value

3. At a premium-to-fair value.

My job was to identify the security, help the client purchase it at
a discount-to-fair value, and hold it until it traded at fair value or
a premium-to-fair value.

To illustrate this concept, I used
a hypothetical "blue jeans"
analogy. It goes like this: If, back in
1990, the average price for a new
pair of blue jeans was $25, my goal
was to buy them at or below $20.
So, I would wait for a sale. If the
new style came out and sold for
$30, I would still wait until they

 Inflation:
A continuing rise
in the price of
goods and services
generally attributable
to the growth in
demand for them.

were on sale for $20 because the average price (fair value) should
have been only $25. Throughout the years, there could be many
factors that adjust these prices, such as **inflation**, a change in the
sales-tax rate, or something related to the product themselves (e.g.,
dye changes, etc.) — any of which could affect the price of the jeans.
These factors might push the average price for fair value to $40 in
2018 dollars. On the other hand, technology and competition may
have dropped the price to the point that the fair value for the blue
jeans was just $20 in 2018 dollars.

In any event, with research, I would work to determine the fair value
of the "blue jeans" (a security) at the time and make purchases below
that threshold. This value orientation worked with both stocks and
bonds. The hard part for "shoppers" is that they must be very patient
to wait for the deal, and sometimes the holding can last a long and
boring time. *As you can see, my approach is very logical, as opposed to
emotional or artistic. I was more interested in finding a bargain than
finding the next new drug, technology or process and hoping it would
be a blockbuster.*

ON THE STREET, SURFERS DON'T LOOK LIKE SHOPPERS.

The contrast to a value-oriented investor is the growth-oriented investor. Growth-oriented investors are like surfers. They troll out in the water, looking for the next great wave and hope to jump on it early and ride it as far and as fast as they can. Then they try to get off the wave safely before it crashes out or fizzles onto the shore. After that, they swim out to troll for the next wave — the next awesome adventure. Speed and distance are the only measures that matter. Emotion, not logic, tends to fuel the waves of growth investors. The investment tides seem to come and go — move and flow — as the next new technology or trend emerges/recedes/re-emerges/recedes yet again. And then the process starts over again in a new industry just a little further up the beach.

There is absolutely nothing wrong with surfers, but I grew up and live in Kentucky. I have seen surfers on television, and I've been to the beach on vacation. I even stood up on a board one lucky day and rode around a little. But I am not a surfer! True surfers live near an ocean. They surf daily. They know the subtleties of the waves. They know when to get on and when to wait. They know what the real dangers are. They are professionals, not guys who come to the beach every couple of years on vacation and try to give it a ride. They are constant thrill seekers. But as experienced as they may be, they inevitably get wet, and sometimes they get hurt — sometimes badly. But good surfing is fun, and even shoppers like to give it a try every now and then.

Likewise, every surfer must go to the grocery store, and even surfers know how to spot a bargain. So, the question for my financial clients was not, "Are you a shopper or a surfer?" but rather, "How much of

each are you?" If the client was much more of a surfer, it was better
that I referred them to professionals who specialized in surfing. That
was not who I was, and our success would have been challenged if
I was to be pressed into that mold. But I was becoming a pretty good
shopper! Of course, there are many other types of investors. Some
could be traders or speculators — true gamblers. Others could be
technicians who just follow patterns. The shopper-surfer spectrum
was just my conversation starting point. Value-oriented clients —
shoppers — were the ones I believed I could help the most.

> *This is where I suggest that you look deeply into yourself and think
> about creating your investment philosophy statement. Are you
> more logical or emotional? Are you assertive or passive? Would you
> rather surf or shop? When prices go down, do you focus on what
> was lost, or do you see an opportunity for a potential bargain?
> Again, these aren't all-or-none questions, but having a feeling of
> your preferences will help you. It will help you relate to the profes-
> sional (or point out where you don't relate with them) and guide
> you to investments that fit you best. But you might need some more
> help to craft out your statement.*

For me, there are several factors that come into any shopping experience and, while budget is certainly a very important component,
quality, price and time were the most important parts of the investment decision to me. Mark Twain was famously purported to have
said, "The return *of* my money is more important than the return *on*
my money." I certainly agree and, as a professional, I only wanted
to work with the best tools — those with the highest quality. The
companies I studied had to have the reputation as the best or second
best in their respective industries. They were the largest companies in
the world. They employed the brightest minds and scholars and were
proven winners. Their leads extended much further than the competition. In financial jargon, they had "wide moats" where competition

and corruption could gain very few footholds. In some cases, their biggest problems were that they were too big and powerful, and needed more governmental intervention to protect the public if their quests for profits resulted in unfair consumer practices or risks.

These companies were household names and immediately recognizable for their brands, products and services. They would be described as fulfilling their clients' needs much more than their wants, but were also very good at fulfilling, if not shaping, the public's desires as well. In the oceans of the markets, these were the biggest fish. These were my tools and, yes, they were the ones that I needed to trust. *What types of tools do you want to own and use?*

The next component of the shopping experience dealt with price. As previously stated, at the beginning of my career, our area of expertise and emphasis was with bonds and utilities stocks. During that time, we focused on the guarantees of the bonds and the necessities of electricity. What could we trust? While stock prices

 Capital Intensive: Requiring much money to secure land and/or rights of way and construct the infrastructure to operate the company's mission.

might rise or fall, we knew with some certainty what the demand for electricity looked like around the world. Utilities were stable, **capital-intensive** companies, and they followed regulations to protect the public's interests in pricing, ecology, sustainability and efficiencies.

The utilities we sought were leaders in their fields, and we focused on those that created electricity, as opposed to those that purchased and remarketed it. These utilities were like spigots from which energy flowed, and their flow was controlled by the cash flows of their

customers and the regulators that determined its pricing. They had
great quality and then the question was, were they priced to potentially give the clients a better rate of return than the bank was willing
to guarantee them given their certain levels of risk over a defined
period? With research, we could determine our estimations of fair
values of the companies, and then start bargain hunting. *"Hold up
Dad, how do you spot a bargain?"*

Great question! If asked to point to a celebrity who might epito-
mize the shopper or value-oriented investor, I would refer to Oprah
Winfrey. There is a page within the Home section of Oprah's website
dedicated to personal finance.[1] There are articles and video clips that
help readers avoid the pitfalls associated with overspending and the
impractical uses of money. There are financial travel tips, as well as
strategies for grocery shopping. At one time, there were even "Money
lessons you don't need to follow." This section is Oprah's attempt
to help people with their money and one area that tries to identify
bargains. If only the investing world would work as well!

**Bargains in the investing world don't generally feel
fun and exciting. They are often accompanied by
fear — and most particularly the fear that whatever
might be wrong might also get worse.**

Bargains in the investing world don't generally feel fun and exciting.
They are often accompanied by fear — and most particularly the fear
that whatever might be wrong might also get worse. At retail stores,
jeans go on sale for many reasons. Maybe the stores are trying to

---

1   http://www.oprah.com/app/personal-finance.html

clear out inventory to make room for new products. Sometimes there are "Scratch and Dent" sales to adjust the value of slightly damaged products. Sometimes stores try to diminish the loss they might incur if they can't sell the product at all. I'm quite certain that Mark Twain would have wanted the return of *some* of his money rather than the loss of *all* of it. *Wouldn't you?*

The financial markets have no such advertised sales. The only advertisement that a security is on sale is that the price of the security has been discounted. It is left to the consumers and the professionals to determine whether it is a bargain, or whether something is inherently wrong with the company. Here, like professional surfers, true shoppers have the advantage of studying these jeans every day and knowing the subtleties of the stores. This is where the financial professionals should be able to truly help you. No shopper would run to the closet, pull out all their jeans, and go to the mall to try to sell them back because there is a sale on blue jeans that day! But in the financial markets, fear and panic can produce exactly that mentality. *(The fear that what might be bad right now might get worse.)* In contrast, if the jeans were of high quality and being offered below their fair value, wouldn't shoppers be looking to buy more of them? *"So Dad, how's that work with investments?"*

Well, there are many ways to determine fair value of a stock but, generally, most of my methods revolved around the earnings of the company. When investing in common stocks, the purchaser of the security is buying a "share," which is an ownership interest in the company. After all the company's revenues are recorded and their expenses are deducted, the resulting earnings are calculated and divided by the number of outstanding shares. From there, the earnings are either paid to the shareholders in the form of a dividend (an actual cash payment to the stock owner), retained for future corporate uses, or some combination of both.

Understanding the nature of these earnings is paramount to finding value. How predictable are the earnings? How long is the product cycle? Is there intense competition within their industry that might displace the earnings at times? Are the earnings growing over time? Are the earnings greater than the bank is willing to guarantee?

Good research over time will reveal most of these answers, but sometimes unexpected events can disrupt a company and affect its earnings. Changes in leadership, focus, product pricing and competition are all factors that can cause disruption. But some factors are only temporary. For example, perhaps there has been an accident that affected delivery schedules. Or maybe the union employees are striking while negotiating their employment terms. *"Yo Dad, kinda feeling deep here. You're stepping back behind the foreign land food counter with some of this jargon."*

It's not that good companies don't have problems; it's how they handle their problems that can make them great.

OK, think about your life. Suppose you've got everything in order and you're just humming along when suddenly you're involved in a car accident. How terrible! Did you get hurt? Was it your fault? Did anyone else get hurt? Is the car totaled? Is it going from bad to worse? Will you ever get to drive again? Were you negligent? Are you a negligent person? Are there going to be many more accidents in your future? Are you really a poor driver, or is this just a fluke? Companies can have similar issues and problems. It's not that good companies don't have problems; it's how they handle their problems that can make them great. Is the company just experiencing an "accident" or are they bad drivers?

There are many ways the earnings could be impacted, but it is generally the relationship between the price of the security with those earnings that just might produce the discounts to fair value necessary to create a bargain — and, as a shopper, that was exactly what I was seeking.

But note: It is most important to remember that the price of the stock reflects the demand for the *stock*, not necessarily the demand for the company's product or services.

It is most important to remember that the price of the stock reflects the demand for the *stock*, not necessarily the demand for the company's product or services.

"Sometimes stocks go up merely because they are going up, and they don't because they don't."

— *Wes Rutledge*

Most of Yogi Berra's famous quotes have a point of truth in them, even if they sound a bit like riddles. While most everyone has heard the adage of "buy low, sell high," nothing in the market system is really that simple. The pricing of the security is not always calculated mathematically or even logically to the earning factors. If earnings are accelerating, sometimes the price might accelerate faster as buyers rush to get on board for the ride. Just as one surfer arrives, so does another, and another — all to catch a great ride, and each pushing the price a little higher. As demand for the security surges, sellers adjust their prices higher to get even higher returns.

Similarly, when news of a difficulty gets out, some sellers may rush to get out before things get worse or the price falls further. Figuring out direction and how to get there are sometimes lost in all the action. The markets can be thought of as a great battle between greed and fear — at each end is great emotion but not always great logic. Sometimes stocks go up merely because they are going up, and they don't because they don't. Sometimes there may be little relationship between a company's stock prices and their earnings. Some stocks go up even though they don't have any earnings at all.

The markets can be thought of as a great battle between greed and fear — at each end is great emotion but not always great logic.

In contrast, during periods where some stocks are increasing rapidly, some stocks may not be advancing at the same rate of speed, if at all. Many times, those companies are overlooked because they are not going up. With low demand for the stock, it does not go up because it is not going up — even though its earnings might actually be increasing, albeit at a slower rate of speed.

"OK Dad, I get it — a little. You said quality, price and time were your most important factors in making investment decisions. What's up with the time factor?"

The time component of an investment can never be overlooked. My investment philosophy statement never lost sight of why people came to invest: to get a better rate of return than the bank was willing to guarantee them given a certain level of risk *over a defined period.*

In the late 1980s, when the markets were skittish, the safety of bonds and utilities eased the fears and risks of bad returns, but in August 1989 , the DJIA had finally surpassed its previous all-time highs. In less than two years, the market had risen more than 30% and, as remarkable as that was, there was much more to follow. By the mid-1990s, the DJIA increased another 1,000 points to close 1994 at just over 3,800. At the end of 1996, it nearly doubled and closed at 6,448.27. At the end of 1998, it closed up an additional 50% increase at nearly 9,200. And at the end of the century, it closed at 10,786.85. They gave out hats and pens and had a real celebration when it closed above 10,000.

So again, if you're keeping score at home — from 1973 to 1983, the DJIA was mostly flat as it flirted with the 1,000-point level. Not much growth for your tree on the corner. From 1983 to 1987, it rose from 1,000 to 2,700 — before falling back to 1,700 with the crash of 1987. From October 1987 through December 1999, it grew from 1,700 to nearly 10,800 — so in about 15 years (end of 1983 through 1999), your tree had gotten about 10 times larger. Impressive!

As fast as the prices were growing, the earnings were increasing at a decent pace, though not nearly as robustly. Interest rates had come down fairly significantly. But as remarkable as the rise in the DJIA had been, its performance at the end of the 1990s was eclipsed by what had been thought of as its little brother, the National Association of Securities Dealers Automated Quotations (NASDAQ). *"What?! There was a faster growing tree?!"* The NASDAQ had been the market for smaller, lower capitalized companies. Its listing require- ments were easier. It did not have the leadership perception of the New York Stock Exchange (NYSE), The DJIA, or the Standard and

Poor's 500 (S&P 500), but it was where many technical companies
would get their start.

Throughout the 1990s, prices increased along with earnings in many
companies. By the late middle of the decade, it was thought that
somehow the world of finance had split into two different investing
realms: The Millennials (also known as the New Economies) and
the Old Economy (OE) stocks. Millennial companies were the new
technology companies that were developing daily. OE stocks referred
to more traditional companies.

Originally, some Millennial companies were developed to deal with
"the Y2K problem" caused by software having been written to show
years with only two digits instead of four (e.g., 1995 was entered as
95). Unless corrected, the code would have read the upcoming turn
of the century as 1900 instead of 2000 — which would cause huge
problems in the future. (A simple example — the kids born in 2005
would be immediately eligible for senior citizen discounts because
the computer would read them as 95-year-olds instead of infants.)

The cost associated with rewriting the code was staggering, and after
exploring the options, most companies and government entities
opted to replace the systems with completely new technologies.
Some of the technologies were being developed at breakneck speeds.
These new, fast, upstart companies would be born and dwell in the
NASDAQ market.

As notably as the DJIA had grown through 1990s, the
NASDAQ's performance, with all its technical company initial public
offerings (IPOs), would dwarf the DJIA. From the end-of-October
1998 close of 1,771.39, the NASDAQ rose to the December 31, 1999,
closing price of 4,069.31. *That little tree grew well over twice its size in
just over a year!*

Companies were spawning and growing like Bermuda grass on a dirt lot in a moist August. People were calling to buy stocks when they had no idea what a stock was. They had heard on TV, been told by their brother /sister /friend /boss /neighbor /cab driver /barber / housepainter /whomever that a stock was going up — and they wanted some too. They had no idea what the company did, and they didn't care. They were buying it because it was going up. *Fast growing trees were sprouting up everywhere!* Quality, price and time were not the public's issues. The speed of making money was all that they wanted. It was a gold rush. Stocks were going up because they were going up, and the surfers were having the rides of their lives. But where was I, the professional shopper?

HOW DO YOU WANT TO BE WRONG?

While the Millennial stocks grew at astounding rates, some of the Old Economy stocks were just trudging along at substellar levels. As the markets were producing 20%+ increases annually, some OE stocks were producing returns in the low to mid-teens or lower. Many bank guarantees were even lower. The main differences between the OE stocks and the Millennials were that the OEs had earnings, earnings predictability and wide moats. Millennials were trading on what they hoped they would achieve based upon their potential sales more than any earnings probabilities. But, again, what was I doing at that time? *"Come on Dad, weren't you playing with some of that, too?"*

Most of my clients had a little exposure to surfing. Occasionally, some of them knew which growth companies they wanted. Every now and then, I had an idea or two about what might do well. But to add growth exposure, we would primarily buy growth mutual funds, which were run by professionals dedicated to that strategy — the professional surfers.

For the most part, I was still shopping for bargains. Some companies were being overlooked because their earnings growth didn't resonate with media — so, they didn't go up! In some cases, people were selling these OEs to buy the Millennials, as if they were just looking for a "faster horse" to get them a quick return. As time progressed, the companies that didn't go up weren't going up because "they don't go up" by shear reputation — not that their earnings weren't growing. This situation produced measurable discounts to value (i.e., bargains).

In December 1996, Alan Greenspan (Chairman of the Federal Reserve at that time) issued this statement:

> "Clearly, sustained low inflation implies less uncertainty about the future, and lower risk premiums imply higher prices of stocks and other earning assets. We can see that in the inverse relation-ship exhibited by price/earnings ratios and the rate of inflation in the past. But how do we know when irrational exuberance has unduly escalated asset values, which then become subject to unexpected and prolonged contractions as they have in Japan over the past decade?"[2]

This "exuberance" would last and intensify for more than three more years. There were plenty of growth opportunities and a few bargains every now and then. All that was needed was cash to buy them.

"So Dad, I'm trying to follow you here. You were talking about having an investment philosophy statement and then you saw a squirrel or something. You then started talking about how the markets were climbing and how you were trying to keep up. Where are you headed with this?"

---

2   "The Challenge of Central Banking in a Democratic Society", 12/05/1996

That is exactly my point, but you've missed it a little. During this period of rapid growth, I was still following my philosophy statement as a shopper — even though the surfers were having the rides of a lifetime. I was trying to get a better return than the bank was guaranteeing over a certain period (not a better return than the markets were providing). My beliefs were grounded in logic and followed a plan, even though growth was exploding. In 1996, Mr. Greenspan was trying to pump the brakes on all this fast growth by calling it "irrational exuberance." Even he couldn't persuade the investing public to calm down because they were getting lost in the emotion. Want to guess how this turns out?

? **Something to Ponder After Chapter 2:** When you sit down with the pro to spend your hard-earned dollars on investments, isn't *how* you invest your money at least equally as important as *why* you invest your money to build your wealth — if not more so? Trust is important, but isn't understanding, too?

Dollars and Sense

Young Adults:

While the first chapter was about developing trust and becoming knowledgeable, this chapter delved into the topics of direction and planning. Direction should be easy — we want things to go UP! Right? But, is it really as simple as going up and not going down? From 1973 through 1983, the Dow Jones Industrial Average and the S&P 500 traded essentially sideways. Why would anyone want to put money into those markets then? "Why" is an easy question to ask, but the answers are never simple. Logic and emotion don't always work hand-in-hand in the world of finance.

In this chapter, we began to think of investments as individual pieces, and collections — rather than just markets. What is it we are shopping for? In times when markets collectively are flat, some companies do better than others. The same is true in "down" markets — and "up" markets, too. It's easy to get lost when everything is going great. Who needs a plan then?

And yet, just before the airplane takes off, and everything is right on schedule, that's when they go over the plans. They tell us what to do in case there is a loss of cabin pressure, decrease in oxygen, how to get out of the emergency exits and what to do if you crash in the water. But there was a plan in place during that great time, too. It addressed when we take off. How fast do we fly? What is our route? But for those of us who've heard these plans many uneventful times, the information just seems flat. Planning

(continued)

and direction: you'll need a sense of both to get where you want to go — whether you're moving up, down or sideways

Influencers:

This chapter is dedicated to direction and planning. Up until now, most all major decisions for the young adults have been made or greatly influenced by you. You took them to a school that you chose (perhaps with their input), put them on the bus, helped them prepare their lunch or made sure that they had money for the cafeteria. When the time came, you helped them head out in the car (or get to the bus stop) and off they went.

But the long and short of it is, they really didn't have to worry too much about where they were going or how to get there — they just got there. Is that the same approach they should take with their retirement accounts, personal savings and investments? Just stick their money in something and hopefully they'll get there, wherever "there" is? When they sit down with a pro, they should work out a plan for how they want to invest their money — as a shopper, or a surfer or some combination of both.

"You've got to be very careful if you don't know where you are going, because you might not get there."

CHAPTER 3

"It's because it's what you love, Ricky. It is who you were born to be. And here you sit, thinking. Well, Ricky Bobby is not a thinker. Ricky Bobby is a driver. He is a doer. And that's what you need to do. You don't need to think. You need to drive. You need speed. You need to go out there, and you need to rev your engine. You need to fire it up. You need to grab a hold of that line between speed and chaos, and you need to wrestle it to the ground like a demon cobra!

And then when fear rises up in your belly, you use it. And you know that fear is powerful, because it has been there for a billion years. And it is good. And you use it. And you ride it; you ride it like a skeleton horse through the gates of hell, and you win, Ricky. You WIN! And you don't win for anybody else. You win for you, you know why? Because a man takes what he wants. He takes it all. And you're a man, aren't you? Aren't you?"

– Susan (Talladega Nights:
The Ballad of Ricky Bobby, 2006)

SPEED AND RULES, NOT SPEED RULES

"So Dad, if growth was sprouting up all over the place, wasn't it pretty easy to beat the bank guarantee? How hard was this if everything was going up?"

From 1997 through 1999, I was seriously being challenged regarding my investment philosophy statement and its practicality in the New Economy. Growth was rampant in the markets. The question was not if the clients were making money. The question was "How much?!" followed by "How fast?!" And there were two other elements fueling returns that added to the excitement: speed and volume. Everything I knew was being questioned, sometimes even by me.

Back in the 1980s, the world of investing and the introduction of computers in the home were also greeted with the dawn of another revolution. Cable TV was expanding and, in 1989, CNBC was created. This channel presented the markets in real time, like never before. Quite literally, the world could watch from home or office the ascent of the markets. And watch they did! As the markets climbed, people would tune in to see how much things went up. The attention seemed to feed upon itself. Things were going up because they were going up and trading was increasing and getting faster.

But, Black Monday had other effects on the world of finance than just market performance. It had exposed a great risk of **default of payment**. In

 Default of Payment: The buyer of a security refuses to make payment for the security purchased.

1987, trades settled in five days. That meant that after an order was entered, accepted and executed, the buyer had five days to make their payment (mail a check, typically) and the seller had to deliver the securities to the firm (either by hand or mail). Security firms and the industry were at great risk. If the buyers just decided not to pay for their purchases (because the security had dropped meaningfully in such a short time), the sellers would be left with the losses. If the sellers had counted on those sale proceeds to fund their own next purchase(s), then their ability to settle the next trade was impacted.

Like throwing a pebble into a calm pond, the effects would spread
a great distance.

*"So Dad, some people just wouldn't pay their bill? What's up with
that?"* Correct again! In late October 1987, there were a few instances
when securities bought by investors might have been down 30% (or
more) before the money was due. While they would eventually be
forced (legally) to make the payment, that process could take many
months (or longer) to resolve.

To reduce these risks, the Securities and Exchanges Commission
moved in 1995 to shorten the time to pay for and deliver stocks
and most securities from five business days to three. This action, in
essence, forced the shares to be deposited with the firms ahead of
the trade by the sellers. They wouldn't have time to go to the bank
to retrieve them and mail the securities. Likewise, the buyers had to
make sure there was cash in the account to pay for their purchases.
By the time an investor received his or her bill, the payment may have
already been late. People began depositing some of their shares and
funds in their accounts, but it wasn't complete or widespread. As
securities and funds were deposited into accounts, the role of the rep
began to shift from securities transactions to securities management.
Coupling a more complete picture of the clients' net worth with the
increased technology and publicity, trading began to grow rapidly.

"In 1995, the year Rule 15c6-1 (the SEC rule which shortened the
securities settlement) became effective, the combined average daily
volume on the New York Stock Exchange (NYSE), American Stock
Exchange ("AMEX"), and National Association of Securities Dealers
Automated Quotation System ("NASDAQ") was 726 million shares.

By the end of 2003, the combined average daily volume for the NYSE and NASDAQ was approximately 3.0 billion shares."[1]

To further ease and speed trading, in 1997 and 1998, Congress began debating the merits of changing how stocks were traded. On April 9, 2001, stocks ceased trading in fractions (1/16ths) and began trading in decimals. The markets were being retooled to handle more trading volume and to move faster. For many people, the allure of the quick return or faster horse loomed large.

As fast as their securities were performing, there were countless other investments performing better. Without proper cash reserves, many investors became traders — the ultimate surfers. The source of the next purchase was the sale of their weaker-performing securities — the slowest horses in their stables, so to speak. In some cases, other surfers would just have to borrow money for the next ride and hope that it would work out as well as the last one! *"So, like I said, Dad, it sounded pretty easy to get a better rate of return than the bank would guarantee. Why not just surf?"*

Fast and quick can have trouble lasting very long and, as quickly as the markets were rising, the reality of the world of finance was becoming evident: No one can spend growth. *"Whoa Dad, if it's worth more money after you bought it, aren't you richer?"*

You could be. But investments can go up and down on any day. What if the security or market drops? Whatever growth you thought you had gained was lost. *"But I thought you said it seemed like every-thing was going up in the late 1990s?"* I did, and yes it was like that in the late 1990s. It was also like that in July 1987 — before the crash on Black Monday. Remember when I said there was a lot of up and

---

1   https://www.sec.gov/rules/concept/33-8398.htm

down movements after the crash? Those movements were important to the development of my investment philosophy statement. So much so that it spawned the second major tenet of my investment philosophy — growth doesn't spend. It must be converted to cash or to something that produces cash to be spendable. Many people think of their investment or retirement accounts as cash balances. They aren't. When someone takes money out of an investment account, they are selling securities and converting the proceeds into cash. Then they remove the cash.

Fast and quick can have trouble lasting very long and, as quickly as the markets were rising, the reality of the world of finance was becoming evident: No one can spend growth.

To me, growth (price appreciation) is not a *real* return; it is a *perceived* return. What was up one day, might be down the next. Interest payments, dividends (earnings that are paid to stock shareholders in cash) and realized capital gains (the cash profit a person receives after they sell a security at a higher price than they bought it) are real returns — they are cash an investor receives. A gain is not a *real* gain until the profit is converted into cash (in financial jargon, the gain was "realized") and likewise a loss is not a *real* loss until the security has been sold at a price below where they bought it, or the company goes out of business. (Yep, the financial jargon term for that is a realized loss — go figure.)

"So help me out with this. Some stocks are designed to pay out cash in the form of a dividend and others are designed to just grow?"
That's right, and some companies also do both.

THE IMPORTANCE OF CASH AND CASH FLOW

Companies, like individuals, ultimately rely on cash and its flow throughout the organization to exist. People need cash to barter for their existence. We pay cash for our food, rent, electricity, clothing, entertainment, education, healthcare, etc. Companies likewise need cash to pay their employees, fulfill their energy needs, buy equipment, do marketing, etc. In the world of finance, cash is blood to the body and fuel to the engine. To build wealth, the system needs cash and cash flow to work optimally.

In the world of finance, cash is blood to the body and fuel to the engine.

As a value-oriented investor, I searched for things that would principally provide tangible, predictable benefits that would give the clients a good probability of getting a better rate of return than the bank was willing to guarantee. As a professional, I was much more interested in having a higher probability of being successful most of the time than having a *possibility* of being extremely successful some of the time. (Sounds like Mark Twain's quote again, doesn't it?)

I wasn't hoping to be "right" with possibilities — I was planning on it with *probabilities*. A strong income stream would provide a probable, real return — which would then provide countless other possibilities. With a good income stream, it is possible to buy a house, a car, a boat, a coat or a vacation home. All kinds of things are possible. You could even buy more investments, and, in those days in the late 1990s, this was where the challenges came in. *"But Dad, if everyone was making money back then how was that challenging?"*

That's a great question, but I was challenged with many more questions back then:

- "Why would I want to buy a bond that pays 7% a year instead of some of XYZ's stock that went up 20% during the past three months?"

- "The ABC stock that you recommended only pays 5%. Why would I want that when I don't even need the income right now?"

- "Why in the world would I want to sell some of my ZOOM stock to buy a tax-free bond that pays 5% each year but doesn't grow?"

- "Why don't we get some more of the new ZOOM stock that went up 50% last month?"

And these are just a few of the hypothetical questions I received during this memorable era.

In periods of high emotion, logic and wisdom don't always reside together. I was relying on what I knew about trust and risk, and another key lesson that I had learned — my investment philosophy's third point: Wealth is built by buying things and protected by selling things.

Positive cash flow (more cash flowing into an account than flowing out) would provide the fuel to allow investors to keep buying the investments. With that cash flow, they could buy XYZ or ZOOM or anything else they might want. They could even set the check on fire and it would not alter the next payment date or amount at all. *"So Dad, money would just flow into the account?"* That's right, and they would get paid while they waited/hoped for the investment to grow. Even more importantly, the cash flow of the investments wasn't dependent on them to do anything to receive it. The investments would keep working, even if the owner retired, went to sleep or died. There weren't other maintenance issues, as if you had bought a rental or vacation house, a farm or some other form of real estate. They don't wear out like a piece of equipment. The money would just flow, and investors could build positions in their portfolios like adding bricks to a brick house or fuel to an engine. *"But Dad, please, how's that challenging?"*

Unfortunately, many investors (and some of my clients) had forgotten the true reason they were investing. While they thought they were trying to get a better rate of return than the bank was willing to guarantee them, they started trying to get a better rate of return than everything else. They wanted to go fast! They wanted a better return than some other high-flying stock or high-percentage bond. They wanted a better return than the market itself produced. They wanted to go faster! They wanted a better return than a different market — the NASDAQ, for instance. Maybe they could get a better return in a different country or continent (Europe, Asia, etc.), which would beat that slow Old Economy company based in the United States. They wanted to go faster than fast! *Hey, speed and volume are fun and exciting — just ask NASCAR.* These investors were quite focused on return but had lost sight and reason with risk. As a professional, I *didn't* abandon foresight and reason, and challenges emerged. *"You keep saying that. Why is this important?"*

OK, let's back up. So far, we've talked about the importance of trust versus risk and forming a direction and plan for our investments. I began laying out my investment philosophy statement (my personal plan) and approach to investing money. They were my guidelines toward putting the money into the accounts. This is important when you first sit down with an investment professional or your HR people and start putting your hard-earned money toward your retirement or other long-term needs. Remember, I started when everything was scary because the markets had just fallen. Emotion was limiting our thinking. Emotion also clouds our thinking when things are zooming along. Who needs a plan then? You're making money, right? *Or, are you?* How do you spend that new wealth, because it is a perceived return, not a spendable return? Will I just have to hope it goes back up if it falls? Maybe, but I'm not gambling or hoping. I'm building, and I'm most concerned with probabilities versus possibilities. As you sit there in the chair (across from your financial advisor or HR representative), are you investing with logic and a plan, or is emotion (either fear or excitement) driving your decisions?

As you sit there in the chair (across from your financial advisor or HR representative), are you investing with logic and a plan, or is emotion (either fear or excitement) driving your decisions?

"But Dad, the accounts were going up!" You're right. But were investors successful because they were smart, or just lucky enough to be putting their money in when emotion was driving things up — because they were going up? And by the way ... congratulations! Now you're challenging me just the same way they were, and this is a good thing. Challenging forces you to think about things. Challenging before you put your dollars into an investment is wise. *"Were those the biggest challenges back then?"*

"The whole is greater than the sum of its parts."

– Aristotle

One of the hardest aspects of my job was helping my clients appropriately measure performance of their securities in the context of their full **portfolios**. In the early years, when the clients had their certificates mailed to them, there were many ways performance could have been distorted that even I might not have known or realized.

Because the certificates were held by the clients, **stock dividends**, **splits** and **divestitures** would be sent directly to them. They may have had more, less or, in some cases, different shares of securities. The truth of the situation was, while I might have had a record of what the client purchased (if it was purchased through my dad or me — and not sold somewhere else),

 Portfolio: A specific, complete collection of investments.

Stock Dividends: Instead of sending owners earnings in the form of cash, they delivered more shares of stock (e.g., 5% additional shares — if you owned 100 shares, they sent you 5 more).

Splits: Some companies thought their stock traded better at lower prices, so they sent out many more shares and adjusted the prices after that (e.g., an owner of 1 share of a $100 stock could have been sent another share and then have 2 shares at $50).

Divesture: Some companies own some (or all) of other companies. Rather than continue to own the shares or sell them, they could just give them to their current shareholders. Then the shareholders would have two companies to keep or sell as they pleased.

sometimes I didn't have an accurate picture of what the client "actually" owned at that time.

Failure to account for the dividend return was another way to distort the measurement. Back then, if a client put their stock or mutual fund on automatic dividend reinvestment (automatically using the cash dividend paid to buy more shares), those new shares were held at another bank. The client never had the additional certificates delivered to them. Comparing performance on price alone was not an accurate measure. There was no single online "dashboard" to consult at this point.

The greatest distortions, however, came when factoring in time. The fact that XYZ paid the client 5% while appreciating another 8% annually over the past four years was lost to the fact that ZOOM went up 50% over the past six months. This is how the conversations progressed. Securities were compared against everything. Growth companies were compared with electric utilities. Small new companies were compared with established Old Economy companies. Stocks were compared with bonds, precious materials (e.g., gold, silver), art, and even more things. Whatever was traveling fastest was getting attention. Moreover, things were being done to try and "soup" up the speeds, or at least make them look like they were moving faster.

Growth (the perceived return) was being measured against everything — and winning handily in the market indexes in 1997, 1998 and 1999. The dance between trust and risk had changed. Speed and volume filled the dance floor. My skills and wisdom were being scrutinized much more than my integrity and honesty. Had I been surpassed by the New Economy because of my belief in the Old Economy system? When Aristotle made his famous statement, was he referring to all his holdings or just the ones his ancient advisor knew about?

"OK, so your investment philosophy statement said that you are a value investor, growth doesn't spend and that you build wealth buying things and protect wealth by selling things. I get that with extra income you can buy more things, but what does that protecting part mean?"

Performance, risk, time, trust, speed, publicity — all of these issues were impacting the world of investing and scrambling investment realities. To sort it out, I had to apply the logic of my investment philosophy statement and adhere to a few other rules I had constructed. In Chapter 2, I outlined my security selection process. Because I believed wealth is built through buying things, I spent considerable time determining what to buy and when to buy it. I was disciplined on the buying of securities and building wealth, and I developed a discipline regarding the selling of the securities I had spent so much time researching and buying. Just as there were only three levels a value-oriented investment could trade (at fair value [FV], a discount to FV, or a premium to FV), I had only three reasons to recommend selling what we bought, and I could never lose sight of the true reason we were investing.

My first reason for recommending that a security be sold had nothing to do with the market, the security or me. The reason resided in the client and their needs. The first reason was that the client needed the money. There were many reasons a client could need to sell a security. Sure, some clients thought that they needed to sell their slower horse to buy a faster horse, but that was much more of a want than a need. The client was making the decision. It was their security and their desire. Sometimes a client needed the money for their own business, or to buy a house, or a vacation home, or a boat/

car/something else. Sometimes a client needed to increase their income with another product. Sometimes a client needed to create a tax loss to offset a gain they had taken earlier in the year (so they wouldn't have to pay as much income tax when April 15th rolled around). Sometimes they needed to reduce a position in a security because its size in their portfolio was creating a bigger risk than they were willing to accept.

Sometimes they knew what they wanted to sell, but many times they would ask for my advice. Which security would have the least impact to their income, their taxes and/or their growth potential overall? How could their portfolio be massaged or tweaked to continue to provide a better return than the bank was willing to guarantee?

"OK Dad, I get that the client might need the money, but why was that the first reason to recommend selling a security, and what does that have to do with protecting wealth?" Those are two good questions. The reason it was the first reason was because it was the client's money and property. If they wanted to use their money and wealth to do something different, who was I to tell them that they couldn't? So, if they needed money, I would work to help them figure out which security to sell and still maintain their income, growth potential and tax status as best as possible. I would work to protect their wealth.

My philosophy's second reason for selling a security had nothing to do with the market or the client. It was based solely on the security. Because I had spent so much time researching the companies, understanding their businesses and their leadership in the industries they represented, and determining their roles within the client's portfolio, I was committed to them. Remember, I was placing my trust, and the trust of the client in me, with these companies. They were the assets of my clients and the tools of my profession.

The second reason I would recommend selling them was if there was a significant change in the operation or management of the company that changed the company into something different than what we had originally bought.

In the 1990s, when the markets started to accelerate rapidly, and everything was being done to push performance, some electric utility companies were striving to keep pace. With all their capital costs and government regulations, many were thought to be the "slowest horses" in the portfolio. To compete, some re-formed themselves into holding companies comprised of "regulated" and "non-regulated" businesses. Some started trading their excess energy production to other needy companies. Some bought the excess power just to turn around and sell it to another company as a broker. Some tried other business forays into airplane leasing and trans-oceanic shipping. The utility industry was not the only industry to try these tactics.

In the late 1990s, some companies even issued "Tracking Stocks" to simulate what the performance of an aspect of a company would trade like *"if"* it had existed as an original stock itself. The tracking stock didn't convey ownership of anything related to the company other than its hypothetical performance "if it had been issued." It was just pure speed — and there were other ways to try to speed up returns. Many companies were looking for an edge, but the edge might just have been the undoing of their company. *"Hold up Dad, what do you mean by that?"* Well, for example, there was a medical company that split itself into two organizations. It put all its services in one company because they were growing like crazy. They put all their buildings and real estate in another company because they weren't growing at the same rate. They thought the buildings were holding the company back in performance. The service company took off and did very well — until there was a change in the rates that the government said they could charge. When suddenly their revenues slowed down, their stock fell. Because all the real assets were in the other company, the service company eventually declared bankruptcy and had to be reorganized — but the stock became worthless. Their quest for speed hurt them badly.

For many companies, the push for extra performance was taking them into areas where they were not the leaders. They were straying from why the client bought them in the first place. For me, they had been selected because they had a reliable income stream or because of their dominance in their particular industries. Suddenly, they were venturing into other areas. How did that impact my client's portfolio? Did I already have other (and perhaps better) investments in those areas?

Each security was selected for a specific purpose within the portfolio so that, when combined with the others, it would hopefully produce a whole greater than the sum of its parts. Would the portfolio have been stronger and better adjusted for risk with these company changes or new companies altogether? Or, was it just a move to push the one part a little faster than it might be designed to go? *So, you sold something if the client needed the money, or if there had been a change in the company. What was the third reason?*

My third reason required the most discipline and, at times, was the hardest reason of all. It often pulled and tugged on the client's emotion and would strain their logic. My third reason was because there had been a rapid, appreciable **rise** in the price of the security over a relatively short time period — but I rarely sold the entire position.

This third reason always came with much friction. "If something is performing so well, why would I want to sell any of it? Shouldn't we be buying more?" "If I sell some of the shares, won't I have to pay capital gains taxes and ultimately have less of a return?" "Why would I want to move from something I know is doing well into something that appears to be struggling or is so different?" "Are we selling it because it is up, or because it is overvalued?"

In the late 1990s, this third reason would test every aspect of my personal philosophy. This pulling/tugging friction that I was dealing with was putting me at odds with my clients. The more I tried to explain my reasons and rationales, the more resistance I ran into. I tried to explain the performance. I tried to help them understand the risks. I tried to talk with them about how the finances failed to make sense in certain instances. But I wasn't making much headway with them. The security was going up, after all! Once again, I concluded that I needed to change how I communicated. It was time to start talking about hair. *"Oh Dad, where's this headed?"* ☺

Most of us remember something of our childhood experience with the barber/stylist. We remember being seated in the swivel chair. Somebody with something sharp was hiding behind us making noises. They placed a tarp over our hands, so we couldn't fight, and mom or dad was right in front of us telling us to be still. They said not to move, or we'd have a bad experience. They assured us that the professional would take care of us and we'd be fine. As we aged, our fears moved away from being nicked, sliced or cut by something sharp to a fear of extremes. "What will it look like if we change styles or colors?" "What if the bangs are too short?" Most of us failed to realize that we were no longer afraid of a physical pain. Getting a haircut doesn't hurt. It can just challenge our mental and emotional well-being. Will it look better or worse? Will it really come back? If the stylist has the right skills, couldn't it be better than we imagine?

And once again "How do I want to be wrong?" came to my mind. At times, the investment world's greatest fears were not how changes would affect the client. It was much more a fear that they would miss out on future gains. I was trying to move our discussions from building wealth to protecting it. We had already accomplished our goal of getting a better return than the bank was willing to guarantee. However, because growth does not spend, it needed to be converted to cash or something that produces cash to make it a real return in our system. This would also diversify and reduce some of the risks that were present but that the client had not fully perceived. It would also give us the opportunity to try to increase the income level of the portfolio and give us more fuel for our engine and more bricks with which we could build.

"So Dad, your third reason for selling a security was really to help investors protect their perceived gains — by making them real, right?" Bingo! Changing the phraseology from *selling* a security that had grown so quickly to giving it a "haircut" was my first step across the bridge with the clients. *Haircuts, after all, don't hurt.* The second step was then relating the haircut analogy to trimming the trees in the yard and then replanting the cuttings to grow new trees to produce even more shade in later years. This would have been especially helpful if something were to happen to that one, great tree. We build by buying things and protect by selling things.

We build by buying things and protect by selling things.

"Wait Dad, in all those years, you never had any other reasons to sell a security?" Correct, I was disciplined. Looking back, I would guess that 80% of the time I was trying to buy securities and build returns. I wanted the money to do the work — build income, build positions,

provide growth opportunities. But at a couple of different points in my career, I weighed very carefully creating a fourth reason to recommend selling a security. March 2000 began the end of the Y2K ride — and even more pronouncedly than I could have imagined.

"WHAT ABOUT CUTTING OUR LOSSES?"

From its peak in March 2000, at the 5,000 level, the NASDAQ plunged more than 3,000 points in 2001 and 2002. Some great big trees were now giant stumps. The common joke at that time was that the 401(k)s had been turned into 201(k)s.

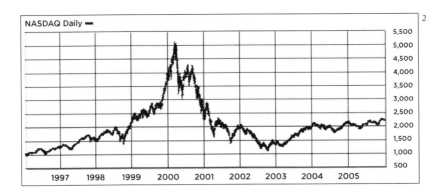

Along the way, there were many times that securities were falling, and we weren't sure of the reasons. Was there something happening in the operation or management of the company that changed the company into something different than what I had originally bought? Was this company-specific or part of a market phenomenon? Should I just jump out and either look elsewhere, or wait and come back later? Should I sell low in fear that it might go lower? If we sell to protect wealth, shouldn't we protect at least some of it?

---

2   NASDAQ, 12/31/1995-12/31/2005, http://bigcharts.marketwatch.com

At that point, we didn't know whether to sell it because it was suddenly thought to be overvalued, or to buy it because it was trading at a discount. If it was down, the question of whether to buy it was challenging our trust with fear. I never added the fourth reason for selling a security because I was afraid it might go down. We were deliberate with what we bought, and we would have good, logical reasons for selling.

"So, Dad, your investment philosophy statement had distinct reasons for buying securities and distinct reasons for selling them. What about the times in between?" Time, history, my dad's advice and my own experience led to two more very important aspects within my statement. First was, "when you don't know what to do, exercise patience until things become clearer." We didn't buy securities because they went down. We bought them because we thought they were trading at a discount to their fair value and would hopefully provide a greater return than the bank was willing to guarantee. We didn't sell securities because they were up. We sold them because we needed the money, something changed in the management of the company, or they had risen to a point where it had produced what we were seeking, and we wanted to protect our performance. This system put us in the mode to buy when lower and sell when higher — as opposed to the opposite.

The second aspect tucked in behind the first. I remember hearing my dad say it the first time early in my career with one of his clients, and then many, many times afterward. After he retired, when I was searching what to do next, he would say, "when you don't know what to do, do nothing and be patient — it'll become clearer" and, "go with what you know — not with what you hope."

Often, when stocks were going up because they were going up, and they weren't because they weren't, we were faced with temptation.

We might be tempted to sell our slower horses. Why were they not performing like the rest of the market? Why was the market skyrocketing without us? These questions put us squarely in the position of when/what to sell versus when/what to buy. Again, were we selling securities because they were trading at a premium to their fair value? Were we buying them because they were trading at a discount? Or, were we buying them because we *hoped* they would perform better than our other holdings?

When the markets were falling, were we selling our securities because we *hoped* they wouldn't keep going down? Were we hunkering down and trying to preserve our wealth, versus investing to get a better rate of return than the bank was willing to guarantee? Indeed, "go with what you know — not with what you hope" helped greatly when we didn't know what to do and being patient until things became clearer kept us from scrambling and making pure surfing decisions. Armed with these rules, we could build wealth. But it was the clients' needs and preferences that led to how we designed and constructed their portfolios.

? **Something to Ponder After Chapter 3:** The first (and unspoken) Law of Nature is that nature has laws — truths to give it shape and direction. Without them, what would anything look like or how would they function? Ask that same question for your investments, unless you would prefer no idea at all (no shape or direction) when planning your financial future.

 # Dollars and Sense

Young Adults:

Chapter 3 was about Speed and Rules. In Chapter 2, I laid out how I approached making investments — from mostly a value-oriented perspective. This approach relies on logic and values. Logic works great until it's challenged by emotion. One emotion that can challenge it is fear. Fear can press Shaggy and Scooby to hide in the barrel.

Chapter 3 goes to the other end of the spectrum to greed. Greed is a sneaky emotion. It cozies up next to you and coaxes you into other thoughts. "OK, I'm getting a better rate of return than the bank is willing to guarantee, but can I get a little more?" "Wait a minute, that other stock is going faster. WTH — that whole other market is going faster?! I must be doing something wrong because mine aren't going as fast enough." "I'm not greedy, I just want more!"

Ricky Bobby knew all too well how great speed can feel. But too much speed can be very dangerous. That's where rules can come in handy. They provide processes and logic when things start moving out of control. When you sit down with the HR people and/or your investment professional, do they have reasons and rationales for how they do things? Do their rules make sense with your plans?

Chapter 3 should also have given you more of a sense of building wealth and protecting wealth, rather than just

(continued)

hoping for wealth. That sense of planning versus hoping should be evolving a little within you.

Influencers:

"Ladies and Gentlemen, Start Your Engines!" Those are truly exciting words — and then the action starts, and everything gets to speeding around. That's when the fun really begins. The excitement builds by the moment. But as influencers, you know that the race is more than one lap around the track. And over a lifetime, there are many races to be run. You also know that it doesn't work out too well if you keep wrecking your car each time you pull out.

Chapter 3 was designed to help young adults develop some action plans toward investing — namely, thoughts of when to buy things and when to sell them. This contrasts with just sticking money into an account and "saving," or plopping it in and hoping it goes up. Sure, it may feel like that month after month with 401(k) retirement plans, but in those accounts, clients can choose to have professional money managers make the decisions for them. What are their reasons and methods for investing their money? Are they shoppers, surfers, some of both or something completely different?

Chapter 3 highlights my methods. Other investment professionals will use other methods. For young adults, understanding those methods and matching them with their own preferences will help them avoid the feeling of getting ripped off if they start witnessing wrecks during the race or start losing control themselves. And sure enough, there'll be another race of sorts tomorrow (and in the next chapter, too).

CHAPTER 4

> So Dad, you had been talking about building returns, and then we got off on a tangent and started talking about being challenged when the markets were taking off. What do you mean, building returns?

"If you can dream it, you can do it. Always remember that this whole thing was started by a mouse."

– Walt Disney

As I came through the late 1980s and '90s, I became more resolved in my investment philosophy statement. I wasn't resolved because I thought it was the best, most complete or the truest form of investing. I was resolved because it gave me and my clients a base and direction from which we could build things. I let my statement become our North Star. As fads and ideas moved through the markets, I became more fixated on my statement. If the client was going to stray from these principles, it wasn't because I just blindly adjusted to the circumstances of the day. Sure, many times the clients wanted to vary how they invested their money. But it wasn't me leading them astray from our reasons for investing. The quest for speed and performance that the public sought had them oftentimes chasing returns like an eight-year-old child trying to catch a greased piglet. The true difference for my clients and me was that we weren't chasing returns, we were building them — together.

The true difference for my clients and me was that we weren't chasing returns, we were building them — together.

With all my rules, it might be easy to think that all my portfolios looked alike. That wasn't the case at all. While they had common traits — and many had common securities — they were each individually crafted to fit each client. Not everyone had the same budget or risk tolerance. The timing of when they had funds available affected the selection of their securities. We were looking for securities that were trading at a discount when they had money to invest — whether it was at the top of the markets, the bottom of the markets or, mostly, somewhere in between. Generally, the designing of a portfolio took more time than picking out its actual securities, but the whole process started with the initial meeting. *"Well Dad, isn't that what you said this book is about — preparing for that first meeting?"* Yep, here it comes.

IT'S TIME TO BEGIN!

At the initial meeting, we generally began with the level of understanding of investments the client possessed. Were they vaguely focused, quite focused, there to win, or did they have other motivations? We talked about the investments they had, if any, and the timing of the needs for their funds. We discussed their savings and cash reserves as preparations for unforeseen events. We explored

their knowledge and control over the investing process, and we
talked about the costs of the investment process. We also were sure to
cover the topic of risks and how they affected returns. But we talked
the *most* about fears!

For inexperienced investors with whom I worked, some of the
greatest fears came from not knowing or understanding how the
investments worked. Did they understand what a bond was? Why
should we look at a municipal bond versus a treasury bond? What
were mutual funds, and why should we consider them? *I know,
I know — more jargon; but don't worry. You don't need to know
what these mean right now. You'll chat about them with your advisor
someday — hopefully, because this book was so helpful, right?* Most
people had some understanding of what a stock was and how it
differed from a bank certificate of deposit or savings account, but
some didn't know how to purchase one, when to pay for it, and
when it would be delivered to them. *"Yes Dad, I can totally relate! But
I'm learning."*

In the late 1980s, the investment process was centered on the
transaction — and, again, the transaction required a high level of
trust. To affect the transaction, the client had to understand the
risks and settlement terms, and acknowledge that a transaction
was being entered. Once an order was entered and completed, the
client was told the price, and the client would then have to submit
their payment — in most cases, by writing a check. Because certificates were being issued, they had to be re-registered in the new
owner's name by yet another corporation. This registration period
would last longer than the settlement period (think in terms of
waiting weeks or months before the certificates were mailed to
the client). The actual trade between the client and the rep at the
time of the trade was really a check from the client in exchange for
a promise to deliver a security sometime soon. It took a good deal of

trust to write a check for thousands of dollars to receive a certificate of ownership "sometime soon" — particularly if the investor wasn't familiar with the process. *"Wait Dad, they really did that? I get antsy if Amazon takes more than a week to ship me my stuff — and I'm not writing checks for thousands of dollars. That sounds crazy."* Crazy, indeed.

By the year 2000, the process had changed to a closer version of today's world. Today funds are deposited into an account and securities and cash are exchanged within three days. The fears of the transaction and its systems had been reduced and shifted to the soundness of the investment; but likewise, the risk shifted from just the performance of the security to the performance of both the security and the account. The security had become a part of something greater, much like a brick is a part of a house.

WHAT DOES YOUR ULTIMATE HOUSE LOOK LIKE?

During my first year, as I studied our largest and most successful accounts, I discovered two clear commonalities among those accounts:

1. They had large positions of securities, and

2. They often held those positions for long periods of time — decades.

Owning 2,000 shares of a company with a market value of $100,000+ or $150,000 invested in a mutual fund or bond seemed a little shocking to me. It wasn't until I pulled the information from my records into a portfolio summary that I realized that the client had much more wealth than I knew. But I didn't always know how many shares they actually owned.

Because the certificates had been sent to the client, sometimes I found that they had even more shares resulting from a previous stock split or other event. For example, my records might have indicated that they bought 1,000 shares of a company many years ago. If the stock had undergone a 2-for-1 stock split, the company would have mailed a certificate for another 1,000 shares directly to the client. Back then, if no one put a note indicating the split into the file, the client actually owned more shares than we had record of them owning.

Clearly, most of these successful investors had not been pure surfers or horse traders. They had built their portfolios over long periods of time — and to sizeable levels. Looking at their accounts was like looking at the plans for Disneyland, where everything was magical and near perfect. But like Disneyland, it wasn't built in a day.

"Walt Disney, born in Chicago in 1901, worked as a commercial artist before setting up a small studio in Los Angeles to produce animated cartoons. In 1928, his short film *Steamboat Willy*, starring the character Mickey Mouse, was a national sensation ... His first feature-length cartoon, *Snow White and the Seven Dwarfs* (1938), took three years to complete and was a great commercial success."

"Why's that significant Dad?" Walt kept plugging away at his cartooning for 10 years before he made his first feature-length film. After *Snow White's* success, he created more films: *Pinocchio, Dumbo, Bambi* and *Fantasia*. Then, he started diversifying — but again, that was 10 years after *Snow White* came out and 20 years after *Steamboat Willy*.

"In the early 1950s, Walt Disney began designing a huge amusement park to be built near Los Angeles ... Disneyland. Walt Disney's metropolis of nostalgia, fantasy, and futurism, opened on July 17, 1955. The $17 million theme park was built on 160 acres of former orange groves in Anaheim, California, and soon brought in staggering profits. Today, Disneyland hosts more than 14 million visitors a year, who spend close to $3 billion."[1]

"Wait Dad, isn't Disney World much bigger than that?" Yes, it is, but it didn't come until much later, and you're missing a little point in there. What took them $17 million and 5 years to initially build is now handling 14 million visitors and $3 billion each year. That investment tree is putting out some serious shade! And the shade it produced was used to make more investments — including the property for Disney World and the other parks Disney owns.

The plans for the creation of Disneyland were woven from the initial creation of a mouse character, to giving him some friends, to creating new characters, and to ultimately giving them a physical home. It was a place where people could come see, touch, play and visit with these characters, and it took many years to complete. But this was just the beginning — the initial investments!

When constructing a theme park, it takes vision, planning, organization, sequencing, and execution (among other components) for a successful endeavor. Building a financial portfolio is no different. Unlike just looking for discounted or trendy bricks and slapping a few together to form a wall of unknown proportions, building a portfolio began with identifying a realistic goal and designing a plan to achieve it. Before my clients needed bricks, they needed a plan — and a sturdy foundation. *"That's like you said we wouldn't just stroll*

---

1   http://www.history.com/this-day-in-history/disneyland-opens

*into Home Depot and start buying lumber without knowing what our
house looked like, right Dad?"* Bravo! You are catching on.

The first part of building the
client's plan dealt with the
client's tolerances and tones,
risks, surfing desires, and immediate fears. Balanced against

 Volatility: Quick,
unpredictable and
meaningful movements.

these were discussions of expectations. In the early part of my career,
the markets' **volatility** and the clients' fear of loss limited some of
their thinking toward returns. Fear was dominating their thinking.
In contrast, later, when the markets were flying, the expectation that
everything would continue zooming along equally distorted views.
That's when our buddy, greed, would stroll in and slide up next to
us and whisper in our ears. Trying to keep the clients focused on
beating the bank guarantees was challenging. Focusing on things that
we could predict, and sticking to our plan, was essential. I worked
hard to direct most of our initial conversations toward predictable
activities.

**The first part of building the client's plan dealt
with the client's tolerances and tones, risks, surfing
desires, and immediate fears. Balanced against
these were discussions of expectations.**

Predicting the price performance of a stock or market over any
short period is extremely difficult. Emotion, logic, supply, demand,
and many internal market factors could each be affecting performance. There could be more than one factor at a time. Ironically, the
market itself could be a factor, even though it was totally unrelated

to the performance of the company. *"What do you mean by that?"* Well, when emotion gets going in the market, and the markets start feeding off of that emotion (either up or down), sometimes individual investments go up just because the markets are going up — or down because they are going down. Just as soon as the factors might align one way, they could shift, flip, and turn in another direction. Those shifting factors make short-term performance hard to predict.

To prosper in this environment, I had to be disciplined and focus on the things I could predict with a reasonably high probability while keeping in mind my real goal wasn't to get a better return than the market would produce today — whenever that particular day was. My goal was to get a better rate of return than the bank was willing to guarantee over a different amount of time. That time was generally measured in years. Focusing on years changed the factors that were most important to us because at the end of any year, we could only really have three general conversations:

- The client's **portfolio** went up, down or sideways

- The client's **income** went up, down or sideways

- The client's **taxes** went up, down or sideways.

These conversations would synthesize my investment philosophy statement. Real (spendable) returns came predictably in the form of cash flow. Reducing the taxability aspects of the account meant that the client could keep more of what they actually received. *"But Dad, isn't the most important conversation the one about the* portfolio *going up, down or sideways?"* Not necessarily, and you need to be very careful with this question. This is where many people start slipping on their investment objectives. If we were investing to get a better rate of return than the bank would guarantee, the price of the security (and its perceived return) is just one piece of the puzzle. That reported price has nothing to do with how much income the security produces and its taxability, as counterintuitive as that might seem.

The securities we were buying to build their wealth were not ones we thought were likely to go up quickly or soon. They weren't purchased because they were climbing rapidly, nor were they purchased so we should turn around and sell them at a profit in the short term. They were purchased because they were trading at what we thought was a discount to what they were worth. It could be a significant amount of time before others saw what we thought created the discount. In most instances, we were very aware of what we were getting paid while we waited for the security to hopefully return to our computed fair value. The truest part of these conversations was that there was no way I could predict with any certainty the performance of an account, but I could predict with a higher probability its income and tax ramifications in a well-diversified portfolio.

"But Dad, doesn't that price and monthly statement tell me how much I'm worth? And if that goes up each month, isn't that better?" This is why I said you have to be careful. You're moving into two sticky areas. *"Wait ... what? Two areas?"* Well, you're heading back into that perceived return versus real return argument, and you're also losing sight of time. Remember the part of the philosophy statement that dealt with investing to get a better rate of return than the bank was willing to pay them ... over a defined period? Was that period one day? One month? One year? Just because your investments might have gone up this past month doesn't mean that they will be up at the end of next month. Or tomorrow. Or next year. Those statements have lots of details in them, and the bottom-line number is just one of the factors that should be considered important. *"You're right Dad, some things do kinda slip up on ya."* I know, that's why I focused more on the cash and cash flow of the accounts. In a diversified account, there

was generally less volatility with those two components and more true predictability.

Just because your investments might have gone up this past month doesn't mean that they will be up at the end of next month. Or tomorrow. Or next year.

After our initial meeting, I would begin scratching and drafting out a proposed portfolio for the client. Rather than concentrating on what the portfolio had in it, I focused on what I could predict it would most probably do — and then look at where some of its potential would originate. If, for example, we were trying to get a 7% average return to beat the bank's 5% five-year CD, a cautious client might want most of the portfolio invested in different bonds with an average rate of 6%, and most of the rest of the portfolio into stocks that paid in dividends. The hope would have been that the stocks would grow 4-5% each year for the next five years on top of what the securities paid. We could calculate how much real return to expect with a fairly high probability. A different, more aggressive investor might have those same securities but have them invested with 25% in the bonds and 75% in the stocks, hoping for more growth versus a lower-level income.

The initial meeting with a new investor gave me a strong indication of how aggressive the client was, in general, and how much risk a client could tolerate in any one security. For most of my stock and/ or bond clients, I tried to limit the exposure of a position (a specific security, i.e., a specific stock, bond, mutual fund, etc.) within their portfolio to no more than about 7%-10%, and my preference was to keep the initial investment limited to no more than 5% of the total

portfolio. *"But Dad, if it was a good investment, why wouldn't you
want more of it?"*

There were three very important reasons for this sizing of positions:

1. A position of this size is statistically relevant to positive perfor-
    mance. If we were correct, and the stock or bond moved as
    we hoped, we would have a large enough position to have
    a meaningful experience. Imagine if a crazy thing happened and
    the stock exceeded our expectations by going up 20% in the first
    six months (and crazier things than this did sometimes occur)
    but our initial position was only 1% of the portfolio. Our success,
    while outstanding, was quite ineffective. In a boxing analogy, we
    had no power in our punch. *(Of course, when you live in Louisville
    KY — the birthplace to Muhammed Ali — you'd have a boxing
    analogy, right?)* While landing the punch squarely on the jaw, it
    would take a lot of these little taps to land a knockout. This little,
    baby position might have been cute and fun, but it wasn't going
    to do any real damage in our make-believe fight.

2. While we were attempting to buy the security at a discount, there
    was no way to be certain that this thought-to-be-undervalued
    security wouldn't trade at an even bigger discount anytime soon.
    While the goal is to buy low, there is no bell or alarm to indicate
    that we bought at the lowest price, and I always wanted to have
    some extra cash in the accounts in case something happened.
    Just like the blue jean analogy, we would hate it if we couldn't buy
    another pair of great jeans if the sale discount became even
    bigger. I'd rather have been wrong with extra money in my pocket,
    than to have spent it all. I'd hate it if the sale got bigger, and I had
    no money to buy more of these jeans, or another good-looking
    jacket that's also on sale, to go with it.

I'd rather have been wrong with extra money in my pocket, than to have spent it all.

---

3. Limiting a position to these levels also would limit the pain if there was any error in our judgment of the reasons for the discount. If we were wrong, the result would sting the portfolio, but not cripple it. The other 95% of the portfolio would not have been at risk this same way. Moreover, there was much more potential that other successes would make up the difference in total performance for the account to offset this one little stinger. Besides, who builds a house with just a few big bricks?

These reasons also pulled us back to that other important element that permeated my investment philosophy statement: Once again, remember from Chapter 2, my conservative nature always asked this simple question:

AGAIN – "HOW DO WE WANT TO BE WRONG?"

"Wait a minute Dad, you mean you doubted what you were investing in?" No, not exactly. No one would be in business very long if they were trying to be wrong. As a professional, I constantly tried to assess and improve returns. One way is to be correct more often. That's always the first goal, but another technique is to lower the probability of being wrong. But there are many ways to be wrong. One way I could have been wrong was in my assessment of the investment or situation. For all the possible reasons of trading at a discount, a company's problems can continue to get worse and

cause it to lose its dominance in its industry. For example, it had been unthinkable to me that a national airline would default on its bonds, and that the county government that issued the bonds to build a wing at the airport would allow the bondholders to lose money as the company descended into bankruptcy. But this actually happened. In other instances, it was hard to watch evolving technologies bypass what were once industry leaders and to witness those former leaders having their capitalization shrink and ultimately finding themselves squeezed out of existence.

Another way I could have been wrong was in the timing of the invest-ment. Even if I was correct in my thinking that the company was sound and undervalued, the situation that caused the discount could last much longer than anticipated. The re-call of the faulty car part might take much longer to resolve, for example.

Another way we could have been wrong was if we bought a security the day before a market adjustment began. I wish we could have known the day before an adjustment or crash began, but it doesn't work that way. Buying a stock one day, and watching it go down the very next day, can make you wonder if you were wrong to buy it in the first place, right? In the short run, maybe we were. Or maybe we might just go shopping again — just like we would for another pair of great jeans marked down even lower.

My objective was to be wrong in the most beneficial ways and to improve with more probable outcomes. To limit the chances of being wrong, I limited the size of the purchase. I concluded that I would rather be wrong with excess cash in the accounts, and look for more opportunities later, than to invest a higher percentage of the funds only to be proven incorrect. Having too much cash in an account (which produced even more excess cash flow) was the way I wanted to be wrong and the best problem I could face. If wrong, we would just have more money to use some other time when the bargains were better, or if there was a great deal to be had on a new car, boat or other prized possession to be had by the client. Sizing the positions at these levels, with a continuous cash flow, put us in position to keep looking for bargains, buying securities and building out positions.

My objective was to be wrong in the most beneficial ways and to improve with more probable outcomes. To limit the chances of being wrong, I limited the size of the purchase. I concluded that I would rather be wrong with excess cash in the accounts, and look for more opportunities later, than to invest a higher percentage of the funds only to be proven incorrect.

This focus on how we wanted to be wrong was a key reason that I tried very hard not to succumb to trading for faster horses. *"Whoa Dad, (get it?!) how does being wrong tie into that faster horse analogy?"* When buying a stock, there are four outcomes that can occur, three of which are not particularly desirable:

1. The stock goes down after we purchase it.

2. The stock does not go up or down for a prolonged period.

3. The stock goes up, but not enough to produce a return greater than the bank is willing to guarantee for our desired period.

4. The stock goes up as hoped or better.

When selling a stock to buy another, the possible outcomes that could produce a negative outcome multiply. The original "slow horse" stock (that was thought to be undervalued) that was sold could correct its

course and move up, while the new stock could move down or not
continue to keep speeding upward. Or, the opposite could happen.
The new stock could suddenly move down and, instead of making
up ground, the losses could get extended. Again, there are many
ways to be wrong. For these reasons, spending ample time up front
researching investments to *buy* is a wise investment in and of itself.
And again, from Chapter 3, we build wealth by buying things and
protect wealth by selling things. Concentrating on how we wanted
to be wrong, if we were to make a mistake, kept us always looking for
another bargain — one that might be even better than before.

This sizing of positions remained generally constant throughout each
portfolio; however, it was modified when using mutual funds and
other highly diversified products. If the client preferred to use these
types of securities instead of making their own decisions, I would
increase the allocations beyond the 5% or even the 10% threshold,
as the client felt appropriate and comfortable. These products had
professional management, professional selection or were limited
to an index. If it was a surfing position of high-tech companies, the
allocation might have been 7%. If it was a conservative growth and
income fund, the position might have been 25%. From my perspective, the key to the allocation was, "How did we want to be wrong?"
When building, it is best not to build with defective bricks.

Like Disney, we would begin building the portfolio with our list of
"characters." We would then add some friends and new characters.
We'd build a house, add some more friends and, before too long,
we'd need to add on to our house or build a second home. Disney
never abandoned its roots: animated film. It built upon them with
a theme park, more animated characters, then more theme parks,
and then network broadcasting. They diversified into an entirely
separate, sports-centered cable franchise system with ESPN and kept
building from there. Today, nearly 90 years later, the Disney dream

has a capital structure of approximately $170 billion (as of December 31, 2018) and they keep adding new characters and producing new animated films. But it all started with a mouse. What a great model to emulate with an investment portfolio!

? **Something to Ponder After Chapter 4:** Why are the first words in the subtitle of this book "Wealth-Building" instead of "Inventing Wealth," "Discovering Wealth," "Witnessing Wealth" or something else? Of those four terms, which is the most probable to occur for every person on the planet? How enticing of a book would this have been if the title was "Hoping for Wealth for Your Lifetime?"

 # Dollars and Sense

Young Adults:

Chapter 4 got us thinking about how to build returns. By now, you may be noticing a little bit of a shift in your own approach toward investing. Are you still flabbergasted by the question, "Do you want to participate in the company 401(k)?" Maybe, or not so much anymore? Sure, it still has the feel of saving money for the future, but by now you might also start thinking about how to build your account.

Are you value-oriented, more of a surfer, or something else altogether? As you first stand in the proverbial HR batter's box, are you still stunned by where to stand and what's about to happen? Or, are you standing in there a little readier for that pitch (question) that's coming?

One way for the account to go up in value is for you to put more money into it. Another way for it to go up is for the securities to go up in value over time. A third, and very important, way for it to advance is to have the securities themselves pay money into your account as you wait for their prices to hopefully go up. Instead of being afraid in that batter's box, are you starting to look for a pitch you might want to try to clobber?

But just because you know a little about where to stand, and that a pitch is going to be thrown, does that mean you ought to swing as wildly and hard as you can in the hopes of getting a hit? Probably not. But congratulations! Your fears have been lessened by learning a little and using logic

(continued)

instead of emotion to guide your thinking. You've started thinking about drawing your mouse and building your house. Next up are a few more tools to make building that house easier.

Influencers:

Yahoo!!! We're about halfway through my efforts to help guide our young adults toward preparing for their financial futures. Hopefully, now they have given some thought to what they are trying to do. Maybe the fear of what happens once they sit down with a financial professional or HR representative has subsided a little and, instead of hoping for things to happen, they are starting to plan a little.

So far, I've used mostly common stock and a few other investments as examples in this book. I've used them so that we can understand some of the materials with which we might try to build our financial homes. Of course, young adults reading this book will have many more products to choose from throughout their lives. But my goal has also been to try to convey a small sense of having their investments work together to fit their needs and preferences. There is more of this discussion to follow but, before we slide into the art of investing, we'll have to go into a little more of the basic realities of math and logic.

Also, there are three, subtle aspects I introduced that you may have noticed. I'll emphasize them more later but, for now, I'm asking readers to think about what something is worth being joined with how much it produces, and how much of what is produced we might get to keep. When building wealth, all of these are important — not just the bottom line number on the statement.

And think probabilities, not just possibilities. It's all about what's *likely* to happen.

CHAPTER 5

> So Dad, even though I'm still a little fuzzy on the investing versus saving, you've been hung up on not being wrong for a little bit. I get that you don't want to be wrong, but why do you keep harping on this?

"Life is a carousel.
It goes up and down.
All U gotta do is just stay on."
– Pharrell Williams

WINDSOR AND ROMANOFF

"So Dad, you said that most people invest to get a better rate of return than the bank is willing guarantee, but you're spending a lot of time on trying not to be wrong. Everybody knows that the markets go up and down, and everyone wants to invest when it's going up, right? Buy low, sell high, right? What's so hard about that?"

If it was only so simple as that, everyone would be rich beyond their dreams. Early in my career, I ran across a brochure that immediately caught my attention. It contained a lesson entitled "Compounding at the Personal Level," which illustrated the concept of how important and powerful a role that simple math plays in building wealth. It was created from a computation simulation created by a service called

Market Logic of Fort Lauderdale, Florida, and told the fictional story of two Harvard men, Windsor and Romanoff (of course their names weren't Andy and Bob, right?), who were both 19 years old.

WINDSOR				ROMANOFF		
Age	Contribution	Year-End Value		Age	Contribution	Year-End Value
19	$2,000	$2,200		19		
20	$2,000	$4,620		20		
21	$2,000	$7,282		21		
22	$2,000	$10,210		22		
23	$2,000	$13,431		23		
24	$2,000	$16,974		24		
25	$2,000	$20,872		25		
26	$2,000	$25,159		26		
27		$27,675		27	$2,000	$2,200
28		$30,442		28	$2,000	$4,620
29		$33,487		29	$2,000	$7,282
30		$36,835		30	$2,000	$10,210
31		$40,519		31	$2,000	$13,431
32		$44,571		32	$2,000	$16,974
33		$49,028		33	$2,000	$20,872
34		$53,930		34	$2,000	$25,159
35		$59,323		35	$2,000	$29,875
36		$65,256		36	$2,000	$35,062
37		$71,781		37	$2,000	$40,769
38		$78,960		38	$2,000	$47,045
39		$86,856		39	$2,000	$53,950
40		$95,541		40	$2,000	$61,545
41		$105,095		41	$2,000	$69,899
42		$115,605		42	$2,000	$79,089
43		$127,165		43	$2,000	$89,198
44		$139,882		44	$2,000	$100,318
45		$153,870		45	$2,000	$112,550
46		$169,257		46	$2,000	$126,005
47		$186,183		47	$2,000	$140,805
48		$204,801		48	$2,000	$157,086
49		$225,281		49	$2,000	$174,995

WINDSOR		
Age	Contribution	Year-End Value
50		$247,809
51		$272,590
52		$299,849
53		$329,834
54		$362,817
55		$399,099
56		$439,009
57		$482,910
58		$531,201
59		$584,321
60		$642,753
61		$707,028
62		$777,731
63		$855,504
64		$941,054
65		$1,035,160

ROMANOFF		
Age	Contribution	Year-End Value
50	$2,000	$194,694
51	$2,000	$216,364
52	$2,000	$240,200
53	$2,000	$266,420
54	$2,000	$295,262
55	$2,000	$326,988
56	$2,000	$361,887
57	$2,000	$400,276
58	$2,000	$442,503
59	$2,000	$488,953
60	$2,000	$540,049
61	$2,000	$596,254
62	$2,000	$658,079
63	$2,000	$726,087
64	$2,000	$800,896
65	$2,000	$883,185

Windsor began investing at the age of 19 and retired at 65. He contributed $2,000 each year to a retirement account (it is especially important to note the type of accounts and the terms of the illustration) for eight years and then stopped making contributions at age 26. It assumed that the investments grew at a 10% constant, annual rate of return. Romanoff, on the other hand, waited until he was 27 to begin his contributions and deposited $2,000 each year for the next 39 years (32 years longer than Windsor was making contributions). His investment returns followed the same, fictitiously assumed returns of Windsor. As the chart shows, Windsor's $16,000 collective investment substantially beat Romanoff's $76,000 total investment. One key to successful investing is centered around time. *"Wow Dad, looks like both guys did pretty good!"*

Yes, it does — but remember that this is a hypothetical example. It shows many things, but it doesn't show everything. Remember back in Chapter 4, where I stated that I was a little surprised by the sizes of the positions as I reviewed our most successful accounts, I should have taken even *more* notice to the length of time the clients had been investing and to the math involved. Most had been investors for long periods of time — decades, or their securities had been inherited from someone who had started investing some time before. This is one of the most important things to be learned about investing. The sooner you start, the longer your money can potentially compound. But also, you'll have more time to attempt to recover from the times where you might have been wrong or recover from times when life gets in your investing way.

The sooner you start, the longer your money can potentially compound.

If both Windsor and Romanoff had died on the same day, how would their accounts have performed had their daughters (in this instance, each had only one child) left them unchanged and continued at the same rates for the next 40 years? Indeed, the power of compounding returns can have a dramatic effect on portfolios. Of course, this illustration only conveys a positive, equal, hypothetical return for both individuals. How would it have differed if, at their deaths, Windsor had five heirs and Romanoff only had one? Or, what if Romanoff's hypothetical wife, Beatrice, had developed severe dementia and he needed to institutionalize her at a great cost to them?

While the illustration shows the power of compounding, it failed to reveal another real aspect of investing that cannot be neglected: Investments don't always go up, and every investor will experience some form of negative performance at some time. This truth is something that my clients and I discussed at our initial meetings.

WELCOME TO WES'S SCHOOL OF BUSINESS. Whenever possible, don't go backward!

In 1992, a foolish day arrived for me. On my 30th birthday, I thought to myself, "Congratulations! You're finally old enough!" I had been a professional for five years and was no longer the student — or so I thought. I had been a part of the worst financial market correction ever and the terrific rebound that followed. If I had only known what was to happen over the *next* 10 years! During that next 10 years, I witnessed the markets climb to dizzying levels as we approached the new millennium — only to see them plunge once more after the turn of the century. "*Yeah Dad, we covered this already, right?*"

Sort of, but you might have missed a little something. The Windsor and Romanoff illustration showed the effects of positive performance but failed to reveal the reality of simple math. The illustration showed basic compounding at the beginning of the period with a positive, constant 10% factor. The world and markets are filled with anything *but* always positive, constant factors. Sometimes the market or a security moves backward. This backward movement can affect returns dramatically in the present state, but can also make forward progress much more difficult — all because of basic math.

In a very basic example, if a client had purchased a fictitious share of stock in the ever-growing BigDollars Corporation for $20 per share and the price then declined to $10 per share, the unrealized loss would have been $10. This would represent a decline of 50% of the initial investment. This statement might be hard for the client to take. "*Yes Dad, half of that hypothetical tree just disappeared!*" Harder to take was that the same $10 stock must go up 100% just to get back to the original investment level. To make matters worse, the time taken on the original investment has been lost, and the assumed gain over that time has been erased as well. While it is possible for an individual to make up performance, it is impossible for them to regain the time. The more time goes by and the return is not made up, the greater the return must be to catch up — and that assumes that it does not continue to go backward. *"What do ya mean by that?"*

Well, if that same original $20 investment in the BigDollars Corp. declined another 50% to the price of $5, it would require a return of more than 300% to eventually get back to the original investment level — even though the stock had only lost 75% of its original value. In our housing construction model, how long would it take to construct a house if the bricks kept falling off walls and disintegrating? *"Defective bricks? Sounds like defective stocks to me, Dad."*

Maybe, but remember stock prices reflect the demand for the stock, but don't necessarily reflect the actual demand for the products or services the companies produce. Those discrepancies can produce the bargains a value investor seeks. When the price of the security goes down, was it because something affected the earnings and dividends of the company? If the earnings and dividends were not affected, was the decline in the stock price reflected as a "real" event? How does the market moving lower really affect a company's operation and profitability? In contrast, if the operations of the company no longer produced enough consistent earnings to maintain the current dividend (which would result in a reduced or eliminated dividend), the loss of income to the shareholder was absolutely a "real" event. The real return (the income level) would go backward. *"So Dad, we're back to that real return versus perceived return argument again?"*

Well, yes, but now there's a little more to add to the lesson. This question of math brings the question of "When do I sell securities?" squarely back to the forefront. Did something in the management of the company change, or was it a temporary phenomenon? Was it performing in conjunction with the market or industry? Should I be selling the security or adding to it? Am I buying to build wealth over time? While the negative math may appear to be large and looming in terms of performance needed to return to the initial investment, another math lesson may offer some help.

TIME TO DOUBLE UP?

By expanding upon the example above, let's imagine that the initial investment for 100 shares of BigDollars Corp. (at $20 per share or $2,000 total investment) dropped to a price of $10 per share (a 50% decline), so that the value of the 100 shares becomes $1,000. It would take a return of more than 100% to get back to a break-even status. If, however, the client thought the decrease was a short-term problem and *added* (bought) an additional 100 shares of BigDollars Corp. at $10 per share, the total cost of the 200 shares of BigDollars Corp. would be $3,000 (the original $2,000 plus the $1,000 for the new shares) and have a total market value of $2,000 (200 shares valued at $10 per share.) At this point, it would only take a 50% increase for the position to get the client back to an even status. BigDollars Corp. stock would need to go to $15 per share instead of $20. (200 shares x $15 per share = $3,000.) *"Wow Dad, that's kinda neat!"*

If the client was more aggressive and bought 200 shares when BigDollars Corp. dropped to $10 per share, the client's investment would have been $4,000 for the 300 shares (100 shares at $20 per share, plus 200 shares at $10 per share.) The 300 shares would have been worth $3,000, and it would only need to increase 33.33% to a price of $13.333 (300 x $13.333 = $3,999) to get the investment back to even status (the $4,000 total investment). The reality of the math is this: the higher the multiple of the shares, the faster the return for the client. *"Hey, you're right. It is going faster. We should buy more at that new price, for sure."*

Be careful, we've already talked about speed. This second math lesson is equally as powerful as the first, but it might be much more dangerous. While the positive potential return might tempt the client, being wrong at that time might have a perceptually more profound effect for the client. Again, how did I want to be wrong? Because my system focused on what we were trying to do as an account in whole and provided a continuous positive cash flow, we could make these decisions at multiple times. We could thereby try to limit the magnitude of how we might have been wrong.

Negative returns also have another, much subtler, effect on people. As outlined above, another thing happened. *"How so, Dad?"* We mentally slipped. We moved our reason for investing from trying to get a better rate of return than the bank was willing to guarantee (which we failed do with this one little part of our portfolio) to a centered thought of what it would take to get back to even. No one in Chapter 1 came to us to invest to get back to even. Indeed, investing with a philosophy statement in mind requires focus and discipline.

Investing with a philosophy statement in mind requires focus and discipline.

AND ONCE AGAIN, RISK POPS UP TO DANCE WITH TRUST.

"Why is that?" Buying a stock because it's down requires trust. Buying more stock when it goes down further, requires even more trust because of a new perceived risk. Now the client has a bigger position — bigger risk. The risk, however, is the client's. It makes no difference to the BigDollars Corp. how many shares an individual owns (provided the client does not own a controlling or dominant position of the company). The BigDollars stock will perform as it performs. The difference for the client is that they will travel 10 times faster if they had increased their initial 100 share position to a total of 1,000 shares. If the 1,000-share position now constituted 20% of the client's portfolio instead of the 2% position that the original shares had occupied, the risk would have been much greater to the portfolio and client. Paying attention to the weighting of the total investment relative to the client's wealth and portfolio was essential. It revealed how much risk the particular client was willing to take. When building a house, it is better to add bricks in rows across the house instead of one large column at a time.

By focusing on getting a better rate of return than the bank is willing to guarantee, we need to understand the true objectives in actual terms — not just percentages. If the security (stock, mutual fund or whatever) had a current market price of $50 and paid dividends equaling a real 2% cash flow, our goal was not to see how fast it would double and get to the $100 level. Of course, that would have been wonderful, but our goal was much more modest. Suppose the bank was offering a CD that paid 5%; we would only need a gain of $5 within a year to produce a 12% perceived, total return. The stock would have increased by 10% ($5) and paid us 2% along the way. If it had only gone up $2.50, our total return would have been 7%

(5% price appreciation plus the 2% dividend return). Both of these examples beat the 5% the bank was willing to guarantee. Similarly, a different $20 security only needed to increase by $2 to produce a 10% perceived return — and then the investor could add on the return produced by the dividend received.

By returning to the true reason we were investing, we were resisting the temptations of our emotion of trying to get back to even. We were returning to logic and probabilities of getting a better return than the bank was willing to guarantee. *You're right Dad, that math does get lost when it gets exciting and things are going up and down in big ways.*

From a market perspective, my focus on value "with a side order of growth every now and then" proved to insulate my clients from devastating losses at certain times. The S&P 500 index did not experience the same losses as the NASDAQ in 2000 and 2001, and many companies with continued earnings recovered while some companies without them went out of business altogether. Clients who had significant cash and bond holdings (and even lower exposure to stocks), in general, didn't watch their accounts decline as much as some aggressive, all NASDAQ stock clients.

My focus on value "with a side order of growth every now and then" proved to insulate my clients from devastating losses at certain times.

Nevertheless, from spring 2000 through mid-2001, the equity markets moved dramatically lower. During that time, we were actively shopping for bargain values. We were trying to buy low with some of the cash we had been accumulating over the previous couple of years. Where possible, at the end of the 1990s, we had been giving our positions haircuts and selling at higher prices because of their rapid price appreciation. We were actively trying to increase the income on the accounts while paying special attention to the client's tax situation. But like I said before, I was being challenged at that time.

Make no mistake ... from 1996 through 1999, I was moving contrary to the market. Stocks were going up because they were going up. Rather than switching to become a surfer or trading for even faster horses, I was actively trying to protect portfolios and convert the perceived returns into real return-producing securities. I was very conscious to determine if the security was trading above fair value or otherwise, but it was extremely hard to operate in that fashion. I wasn't always successful, and in one case I floundered mightily. *"How so, Dad?"*

In March 2000, I received an account transfer notice from one of my larger accounts. I was being replaced as their financial consultant. For three years, I had been trying to defend my philosophies to this client and his wife, but I feared they were losing faith in me and my system.

In the early 1990s, they had been referred to me by their lawyer who they trusted greatly. They had received a settlement check from a lawsuit and wanted to purchase a larger home. The goal was to have the mortgage paid off in seven to 10 years, which put the mortgage payment at just under $7,000 per month. I structured their portfolio to provide them with the income they needed while providing potential for both additional growth and growth of their income. Through the decade, the portfolio performed as we had hoped. By the end on the 1990s they had paid off their home and the portfolio was now generating free cash well over the $7,000 they required. Their securities had gone up in value as well, but not at the same rate as the NASDAQ.

Over that same period, the clients had investments in their corporate retirement accounts with another firm. In these accounts, they had been investing almost exclusively in technology stocks and the most current trends. Their retirement accounts were soaring, but the accounts they had with me were not showing anything close to that kind of performance. Every month, we removed $7,000 from their account and sent it to their bank checking account. I tried in vain to explain that their portfolio performance was being distorted. They were taking money out of their taxable account they had with me to buy their house. The account with me had negative performance, in part because they were taking money (a real negative return, not a perceived one) out of their account and using it to pay off their house. They were causing it to go backward a bit. Another factor was distorting their performance. The account they had with me was not a tax-deferred, retirement account. We had to pay taxes on the income from it and it was subject to taxes for securities we sold for a profit. *Remember when I told you to pay attention to the Windsor and Romanoff accounts because they were tax advantaged accounts — they wouldn't have to pay income taxes until they took money out. In the hypothetical, they never took any money out, so they never paid any taxes.* For a long time, my clients didn't recognize that their wealth had increased by the value of their house because it wasn't listed on their monthly statement.

When the house was paid off, they questioned whether the portfolio should be reconstructed primarily for growth instead of growth and income. My arguments against such a move were that 1.) There were no true valuations that we could determine on many of the tech companies, so we didn't know if we were buying them at a discount, a premium or a fair market value. 2.) By selling the securities, the clients would lose a predictable, real return — the income stream we had created. 3.) They would incur capital gains for which they would incur more tax liabilities (i.e., they *would* move backward), and 4.) It would be expensive for them to do as they wished. (Add some more backward performance.)

Instead, I proposed that they use the free cash that was being generated to purchase the exciting new technology securities in limited and measured ways. If wrong with such purchases, our losses would be limited. In the racehorse analogy, I had been riding a mule. In the surfing analogy, I was being a lifeguard. In real life, I got canned. They transferred their assets to the other firm and sold everything to cover their purchases in the new technologies.

I was truly saddened for them when the Y2K bubble popped in the weeks that followed. They not only went severely backward in pricing, but they also lost the real return of the income stream we had built them. *"Ouch!"* Their investment engines no longer had constant fuel to help them keep running. With a much lower capital level, they could not undo their actions and reinstate their previous positions or income level.

In their eyes, I had been wrong for three years but, from my perspective, it was the way I wanted to be wrong. While we weren't running with the fastest horses, we were achieving a better return than the bank was willing to guarantee. And we were doing so with more probability than just hoping that what was going up would continue to go up. I wasn't happy at all to eventually become correct at their expense during the spring of 2000.

JUST A LITTLE MORE MATH

Negative returns to an account are inevitable. The Windsor and Romanoff illustration was performed on a net-after-cost basis. It didn't consider the fees or commissions paid to buy or maintain the investments. It was done in retirement accounts, where taxes don't come into play until money is removed. In the illustration, they never removed any of their assets, and thus never paid any taxes. It assumed that both Windsor and Romanoff did nothing else or left the retirement accounts to their former spouses or other heir(s). They had no negative returns. Negative returns in investment of some sort are inevitable over time. The key is to try to limit them. The goal is "Whenever possible, don't go backward!" In these cases, it is important to judge whether the movement is moving backward in a real fashion or just a perceived fashion.

In some portfolios, where individual securities were held for decades, **capital gains taxes** were deferred until the gains were realized. Because there were no capital gains realized during the holding period, there was no negative return from capital gains taxes that were paid. This avoidance of taxes

 Capital Gains Taxes: The Federal and most State governments require that taxes be paid when securities are sold at a profit. The amount owed is calculated as a percentage of the gain. Each state has its own policy on taxes.

explains why many investors didn't want to trigger the capital gain at certain times, even though the underlying soundness of the security might be deteriorating. Sometimes, they thought they'd go backward by paying taxes on the gain. Instead, they hoped the company would get better in the future. *Hmm, is my dad's old saying of "go with what you know, not with what you hope" coming back to visit you?*

Selling the security can undoubtedly move the value of the security backward in a real fashion. For example, if the capital gain tax rate for their tax bracket was 30%, and the security appreciated to the point that 90% of the market value was an unrealized gain, then the cost of protecting the gain was great. In commissionable accounts, it would cost a commission to sell the stock or bond, another commission to buy the next investment, and then the tax would be due at tax time. Assuming a 2% commission on each transaction, the actual cost to the hypothetical client could have been nearly 30% in fees and taxes. The return required to get back to even on the next security would be more than 42%. See table below.

Current Total Market Value		**$10,000.00**
Less 2% Commission on Sale		*($200.00)*
Subtotal		$9,800.00
Less Original Investment	$1,000.00	
Realized Gain	**$8,800.00**	
Less 30% Capital Gain Tax		*($2,640.00)*
Subtotal		$7,160.00
Less 2% Commission on Buy of Next Security		*($143.20)*
Remaining Funds Invested		$7,016.80
% of Current Total Market Value		70.17%
Reduction of Value (%) of Current Value (aka Negative Return)		-29.83%
Return Necessary to Get Back to $10,000		$2,983.20
Return Necessary as a % of Remaining Funds		**42.52%**

The question then became: "What is the probability that new investment(s) will recuperate the lost return we paid in taxes and fees, and how soon will it occur?" Jumping on what is thought to be a faster horse when it must catch up by more than 42% — just to get back to even at the start of the race — should cause a client to pause and think for a while. And once again, I would ask myself the following questions:

"How do I want to be wrong?"

"What is my goal toward investing?"

"Am I protecting wealth accumulated, or just looking for a faster horse?"

"What is the probability of success with my next move?"

"Am I increasing the client's cash flow?"

"Am I working with what I know or what I hope?"

Another form of negative return on some accounts might have been margin interest expense — but I generally stayed away from this concept. In the world of finance, people can borrow money by offering some of their securities to serve as guarantees to pay the money back. Interest is calculated and charged as an expense to the accounts, and defined capital levels must be maintained while the loans exist. This margin interest expense is "real" negative return, not a perceived return. It increases the pressure of the purchased security to perform and adds an even greater factor of risk. While it may seem tempting to borrow money at a low level because you believe some new security is deeply discounted or a zooming growth stock, the negative costs of the purchase put new and different pressures on the account. (See table above and add more negative return, known as interest expense, to the purchase. OUCH!)

"Are there any other types of "sliding backward" I might need to think about, Dad?" Negotiating lower fees or commissions that you're paying might be another way to reduce the negative performance — but be very careful with this approach. First, a client should understand the extent to which the fees or charges play on the entire portfolio. Are they statistically relevant? Second, if investment professionals are beneficial, and are working to help you, do you want to start reducing their compensation when you need them most? From their perspective, will they find your desire to cut their compensation beneficial to your relationship? Certainly, ask yourself, "Was engaging them a wise investment, in and of itself? Were the fees or commissions fair and reasonable for the services they rendered?" Remember, like taxes, fees or commissions are paid from your real dollars — not perceived dollars.

Negative returns in an account are inevitable. There are negative prices at times, fees and/or commissions, taxes, margin interest expense (possibly), and other factors. They can be caused by the market, the security or the client themselves. Merely removing assets to fund education, healthcare, leisure or other types of expenses, or to make different types of investments (e.g., real estate or private investments into a client's business or profession) will alter the performance of an account. Divorce, joint ownership changes, and distributions to heirs or beneficiaries are other forms of negative returns to accounts. Winsor's fake heirs had to divide everything by five when he died. And poor Romanoff's only daughter didn't get much after paying all her mother's dementia bills, either. Negatives happen! To build wealth over extended periods, limiting when and how you go backward will go a long way toward arriving at your destination. But just as the math needed to be explored more deeply, so does the element of *time.*

"Wow Dad, that was a lot to digest in this Chapter!" You're right, it was. Hopefully you picked up on the fact that my client story took you through each chapter of the first half of this book. The clients were referred to me, and we were investing for a purpose — yet at times we had trouble communicating with each other. We established and set a direction and planned a route. The skyrocketing markets pulled the elements of trust and communication to the forefront once again, and speed challenged my rules. I talked about how the portfolio was constructed, and it was built to keep building in a predictable way. And then there were the lessons of math and going backward. Yep, we covered each chapter, so far, and yes it was a true story.

"But Dad, that client fired you because you didn't do what they wanted. That wasn't good." That's not quite an accurate statement, and it reaffirms why I wrote this book for you. I did exactly what they asked me to do. We built a portfolio that would accomplish what they wanted. I was a shopper and would've added some surfing with the excess funds. They switched over and wanted to surf even more than they had been doing. I was fired, but it was because I wouldn't switch my methodology to fit them. That wasn't a way I wanted to be wrong. If I just pretended to be a surfer to keep them as a client, I would've been very wrong. I couldn't help them very well that way, and I knew it, and that leads us back to why I wrote this book for you. Hopefully after reading these first few chapters you're starting to feel better prepared to begin talking with the investment professionals — instead of just "sticking it in and hoping everything turns out well." The communication necessary between you and your financial professional is more than "cut to the chase and tell me what to do."

? **Something to Ponder After Chapter 5:** How much faster and further could you go if you never took the reverse step in the phrase: "Two Steps Forward, One Step Back?"

 # Dollars and Sense

Young Adults:

Whew! Chapter 5 sure could seem a little draining. All we talked about was what happens when investments go down. That's not fun or very nice! Why would a book on investing spend so much time on being wrong or going backward? Nobody wants that.

But unfortunately, negative performance happens. Sometimes it's caused by the market(s), a company or some other outside factor, like the government or a foreign issue. Sometimes it's caused by our own needs or wants — to pay medical expenses or buy a vacation home. Whatever the cause, understanding how the math can work should help you a little when you find yourself in these positions. But like I said before, it is highly probable that you are going to find yourself in this spot sometime down the road.

Also, this is generally the root of most fears identified on the very first page of this book. The fear of being ripped off or doing something dumb with your investments generally manifests itself when the account is down from a previous value. What happened to my money? Why did it go down? How long before it goes back up to where it was before? That dance between trust and risk sure sucks when everything is going down. Or does it? By planning on being wrong sometime in the future, and going against the emotion of the day, have we actually set ourselves up to be buying when prices are low with the cash that we accumulated when prices were higher?

Getting ripped off doesn't come from just going down. It comes from being misled. It comes from outrageous fees. It comes from not explaining things fully or adequately identifying the risks of the investment(s). It stems from neglect and/or deception. That's why the first chapter centered on building trust. By understanding a little bit about going backward and how to be wrong, hopefully this chapter will help you move forward over time.

Influencers:

Math (Ugh!) — I'm sorry. I know, for many people, this can seem like a dirty, little word. The mixing of numbers and words can make your head rattle and drive some to skip to another chapter for something lighter or a little easier to work with. But this chapter isn't about algebra, calculus, geometry or trigonometry. Most every student has studied some or all these forms of math during their high school or college learning careers.

Unfortunately, when we, the professionals, work with money and investments, we blend math and language in many ways. We talk about probabilities and possibilities. Sometimes we go into advanced mathematics looking for even more advantages. Standard deviations, variances and even more exotic forms of math are sometimes used to help deliver more performance. But often we forget to go over some of the most basic aspects of simple math. Yes, our young adults have been introduced to algebra, but when were they introduced to the concepts and dangers of going backward? Do they really understand that multiplying the size of the position really can affect the speed at which it performs for them? Is it best that they start truly

(continued)

understanding this simple math with their money — the money that they'll need to support themselves to maintain their living standards when they no longer work?

But understanding math is important in our daily lives — it's why they study various forms of it for at least 12 years. And even though we don't all love working with it, it is necessary for our daily lives. Failure to understand some of the most basic premises can leave us frustrated, angry, confused and, somehow, maybe even exploited — the fears identified on the very first page of this book. Understanding a little more math when our young adults first sit down with investment professionals will help them as they start to build their accounts — as opposed to just sticking some money in and hoping it goes up — and hoping that it's a big enough pile when they want to retire. As Pharrell Williams said, "Life is a carousel ... All you gotta do is stay on." But what wasn't said is that if you have an idea how to handle the ups and downs, you'll have a better ride — especially that first trip around.

CHAPTER 6

**"You may delay, but time will not."
"Time is money."
"Lost time is never found again."**

– Benjamin Franklin

WHAT DO YOU HAVE TIME TO DO? MAKE TIME TO THINK. TAKE TIME TO LISTEN.

"You're bringing up a good topic, Dad — Time. You've given us a lot to think about with the first half of this book, but it still seems like it takes a lot of time to do this investment stuff. How do we juggle it, our careers and our lives all at the same time?"

This book is designed for you and these specific questions. Its purpose is to help you navigate time. The earlier you're exposed to some of the lessons I've offered here, the further they will carry you into the future. Retired people often told me they wished they had learned some of these very lessons when they were younger. Many had no idea what they were doing or why, and very few liked it that way.

Risk and fear paralyzed some of them to the point that they couldn't make decisions. Some people were just too busy to pay attention to important things in their lives. If you think about it, exercise, nutrition, stress management and genetics are all factors of health. Some people are too busy for them, too — but most everyone would agree that managing them with a plan and sound philosophy would improve their results over time. Likewise, creating an investment philosophy statement, drafting a plan, adjusting it along the way, and paying attention to the details (especially of math and time) are helpful to building wealth.

My initial meetings took time. Not all clients appreciated the time they took — at the beginning. As you're now aware, we talked about a lot of things during these early meetings. In the initial meeting, the client was guided to make time to think about how my system worked and how it might be adopted by them. I focused on listening to their answers, so I could do my best to help them. By spending this much time up front with the new client, I was trying to help save time in the future. The first investment that was needed to be made was some element of time. This lesson remained true throughout my career. *"Really, Dad?"*

Yes, but it wasn't always easy, if you can imagine. I can distinctly remember the first meetings I had mid-way in my career with a client of mine. He was a doctor who had moved into our town. One of my clients had referred him to me because we had a good relationship, good performance and our costs were reasonable. That's exactly what I was trying to deliver, but Doc hadn't built his wealth that way.

Doc was a busy man. He'd been investing for many years and had worked with several other "professionals." He'd been so engaged with his investments that he'd been doing it online by himself for several years. He had many accounts spread out all over the place — so many that he wasn't sure how much of anything he owned. Some things were performing very well, but some investments weren't. Most all of them were ideas he had read about in different publications. Remember when I told you about clients who had their certificates in the bank and didn't know how many shares they owned? Well, he was like that — except his securities were being held at several different security firms, and back then he couldn't access the details via online dashboards — they didn't exist then, and he wasn't organized and disciplined enough to do so if they had.

At our first meeting, I asked him a stumper of a double-question. I asked: "What can you predict from your portfolios, and how likely are those predictions?" He didn't have time for my strange questions. In fact, he told me that I'd have six minutes to talk with him before his next patient was to arrive. And, that's the way our meetings went the first half of the year or so. Six-minute meetings.

I could sense he was getting frustrated with me after our third or fourth meeting. In each of those six-minute meetings, all I could do was ask a question or two about what he was trying to accomplish or why he held certain investments. In some cases, I was just trying to keep track of where it was located. Sometimes weeks and months went by between appointments because our schedules wouldn't match up.

Finally, on about the fifth visit, he asked why couldn't he just give me copies of his statements and let me figure it out myself? We'd been meeting for about nine months, and now he finally trusted me enough to offer his statements. All that time, he'd been waiting for me to try to sell him something, and yet all I was trying to do was understand and help him. He told me that he would like my thoughts at our next six-minute meeting. I told him that wouldn't be possible.

Here's why. His statements were complex. He had many different types of accounts: retirement accounts, his personal account, a joint account with his wife, her account (which he had authority to manage), and a few more. When I finished trying to mentally assemble them together, they totaled more than $3 million. Even with all the statements, I would need more than six minutes to help him. I told him the next investment he'd need to make — the first investment with me — would be more time. It would take time for me to help him.

But Doc wasn't the only person to approach investments that way. Many, many other people approached their investments in similar ways. They'd spend hours and days studying and researching new and used cars. They'd look at cars in parking lots and show rooms. Then, they'd test drive them. They'd do the same things with their home purchases. Ironically, when it came to spending time thinking and learning about building their wealth or planning their retirement life, they'd use the opposite approach. Either they didn't understand it, or their emotions couldn't tolerate the conversations. In either case, many wanted to get through the conversation as quickly as possible.

"You've got that right, Dad!" Oh yeah, I remember that, too — you proclaiming in the first chapter that you don't have 27 years to learn this? Hoping that you could learn most everything in less than 27 months, or 27 weeks or possibly less than 27 days? See, we're trying to beat those times, right? But, that's OK and pretty normal for all people. Many times, we address things we don't understand or are afraid of by trying to move away or going through them quickly. It makes us feel uncomfortable and we're ready to move to simpler, easier, less frightening subjects. Just ask Shaggy and Scooby. But in all honesty, we, as professionals, weren't always good at helping our clients learn and work with their investments.

IS MY PROFESSIONAL AN ADVISOR OR JUST ANOTHER SALESPERSON?

During the first 20 years of my career, the business of financial services changed dramatically and, in many ways, so did the role of the financial representative. Just as my personal efforts moved away from being centered on sales transactions and became more holistic to the client's total picture, so did the industry. Through that course of time, products evolved, changed and broadened. Stocks, bonds, mutual funds, options and insurance products were joined with hybrid securities, index funds, Exchange Traded Funds and other new offerings. Using these various products required more education by the professionals, and our careers became more complicated. The changing tax times, world economics and evolving technologies added other elements that drew attention, and these elements were tested and promoted by many institutional investment firms. Mix in a daily television program to add further introductions and attention, and it became much clearer that the role of the rep had truly evolved from a securities sales professional into a financial consultant. *Or had it?*

Through that period, the public perception of consultants may have still tended to be negative through the eyes of some. With existing clients, the trust I had spent years building had placed me squarely in the role of advisor. However, as I sat down with prospective clients and referrals, I often felt that familiar twinge I had experienced in my early days where the client was afraid I might be giving them a sales pitch.

Given the performance of the markets over the years, many of my prospects had varied levels of success, so they were seeking help, advice or performance from other sources. Some had been burned

— either by the markets or by other advisors. Just as the way in which securities were traded had changed, so had the way they were managed and presented. Technology that was used to help analyze and select securities was equally efficient at advancing the presentation of the portfolio strategies and recommendations. In short, as our tools advanced, so did our sales presentation abilities. *"Dad, this is great, but how does it fit in with the first part of the chapter?"*

Well, let's back up a half step. Financial professionals deliver services to their clients. Some of their clients recommend that their friends or relatives use the same professional they have come to trust. (This prospective client is known as a referral.) But sometimes referrals aren't enough and financial advisors must actively work to attract other new clients. Perhaps they use cold-calling, knocking on doors, advertising in traditional or digital ways, or now using different forms of social media to tell stories and make themselves known. When participating in these types of promotional activities, financial advisors can act more like sales people, and this can put prospects on edge.

Trying to figure out whether a presentation was truly in their best interests or just a sales tactic to make a commission was never a waste of time for the client, by any means. No, it was essential from my perspective, but it took time. It would also add a distraction and slow the client down as they reevaluated their philosophy statement and plan. Again, this was not a bad exercise; it would just affect time. My job had become a bit tougher.

My relationship with Doc changed after that awkward "it's gonna take more than six minutes" conversation. When we got to his real goals and fears (and what he was really trying to do) he started extending me more trust. He figured out that I wasn't just trying to sell him something. He found out that I was trying to help him. He found

out that I cared about him and, as he did, our conversations lasted
a little longer and they went beyond investments. We talked about his
children, his brother and sister, his practice, where he vacationed and
how he wanted to live. We shifted our meeting times to lunch time,
and then we really enjoyed our time together.

*"Okay, Okay Dad, I get it. Investing takes time. It takes a plan, and
then we stick the money into our chosen investments, and wait for it
to grow, or whatever, right? That's why we get a pro to help us. They'll
do all the work, right?"* Well, there are two factors that can come into
play that can potentially screw everything up for you — distractions
and when the world changes on you. *"You've talked a little about
distractions — when things slip up on you — is that what you're
talking about, again?"*

IT'S GAME TIME!

Of course, my answer to that question is more complex than a simple
"yes" or "no." Sometimes distractions slip up on you, and sometimes they just storm in on you. Distractions came in many forms,
and there were times when I could swear that clients were craving
the distractions instead of tuning them out. When I started in 1987,
financial news reporting was conveyed principally through print via
newspapers and magazines, but in 1989 cable television brought Wall
Street into the room with the clients and me. (I know, it was almost
caveman-like to not have a smart phone and Twitter to keep us up to
date, like today.)

At first it seemed to be a novelty — CNBC was born! It was news with
a different feel. It was current, it was business, and it was action! It
brought stories of companies that were doing well and those that
were struggling. It introduced new technologies and translated

financial jargon into stories the public could understand. It was delivered with interesting statistics, charts and graphs. The people who told the stories were polished and well-spoken. The format resembled a sporting event. There were pre-game (pre-market opening) stories about the companies believed to be the stars or duds of the day. A timeclock was used to count down to the tip of the day where the opening bell was rung, and trading began. The early leaders were noted for their strong or weak performances, and at lunch time the first half of the day was reviewed.

The second half told more evolving stories and led into the final hour of trading. Again, the timer was used to count down the final minutes of trading for the day and then, afterward, the commentators recapped the day's activities. There was always drama and action. A "crawler" scrolled by on the lower third of the screen, to help keep viewers informed in case they might have missed something. It still works very similarly that way today.

In those early days, I pressed to put a television in my office to carry the show. Clients had been calling me to chat about ideas that were mentioned in the programs, and I had no idea what they were talking about. They heard things that enticed or intrigued them — concerned and scared them — and things they didn't understand, which needed my explanations.

Like most of my clients, I found the information to be very helpful to my practice in many ways, but my reasons were different from my clients! I would discern whether the financial pundits were giving information that would follow my investment philosophy statement, or if their shows were just pointing out where better surfing and faster horses could be found. I had to figure out whether the information was an aid or a distraction. Many times, it seemed to me to be some of both.

In the late 1990s, CNBC (and another new channel — MSNBC) told
of superstar performances of some companies. As word spread that
companies were soaring, more of my clients and friends tuned in.
When the markets began falling after the turn of the century and the
puncturing of the Y2K bubble, some of my clients tuned in to see how
they were affected personally. On September 11, 2001, we watched
in horror as the twin towers of the World Trade Center in New York
crumbled, and as reports from Washington, DC, and Pennsylvania
showed us terrorism like we had never seen before. In 2007, fear
began gripping my clients again, and the dance between risk and
trust went into high gear once more at the tip of The Great Recession.
Through it all, television coverage of domestic and international
markets had significant impact on investors and on those who
served them.

Aside from the distractions caused by media coverage, it
wasn't unusual for investors to be distracted by a call from another
rep or consultant, probing to see if the investor was happy and
satisfied with their current financial advisor, or if there might be
an opportunity for a new person to make a presentation or offer
a different opinion. Sometimes they led with probing needs questions. Other times, they led with what they thought was a good
investment opportunity. Was this what you needed at that time, or
just a distraction? A sales pitch or an offer from another professional
to help you? Maybe some of both?

Distractions! How did these activities — and the fears that tagged
along with them — affect our electricity usage, energy use, food
consumption, basic computing needs, etc.? Would they change how
often people brushed their teeth or took their medications? How did
they affect the incomes the portfolios were producing? There were
instances when I told some of my clients that the best investment
advice I had for them was to turn the television off and go fishing or

shopping for a while. The distractions were creating more fears than positive inspirations or reassurances. Our investment philosophy statement was guiding our actions, and we were attempting to build wealth to survive these events and last a lifetime.

But once again in 2007, the world changed on us and we were challenged with our performance. *"Wait Dad, wasn't 2007 the year when things got really scary — like maybe we were heading for another Depression or something? Is that what you mean by saying that the world changed, and that changes in the world can screw you up, time-wise?"* Yes, if I had learned much during my first 15 years in my profession, the next five years (from 2002 to 2007) confirmed that my investment philosophy statement had been working. But 2007 was different, yet again.

In 2007, everything abruptly changed. Nearly everything in the business world came to a screeching halt. Banks were going into bankruptcy. Companies were closing. People were losing their jobs and being forced to sell their houses. Everything seemed to be going down in price. The worst economic period next to the Great Depression of the 1930s was unfolding. While it didn't reach the same levels as the Depression era, the fear and impact of 20007 were so great that it was named the Great Recession.

In 2007, everything abruptly changed. Nearly everything in the business world came to a screeching halt. Banks were going into bankruptcy. Companies were closing. People were losing their jobs and being forced to sell their houses.

The Great Recession descended upon the country, and its entry into the clients' lives was also different to many of my clients than previous financial crises. While television still brought Wall Street into their homes and offices, computers and new technologies would focus their attention to their own portfolios and holdings. The news that came through these means could be tailored to the clients' very specific circumstances. People didn't have to wait for their monthly statements to see the true impact of the day's activities. They didn't have to call their financial professionals to get information. They could get it anytime they wanted — and sometimes faster than the professional could deliver it themselves. News and distractions had become ever-present and faster, and my role had evolved even more.

From 2002 through 2007, the financial markets recovered from the Y2K bubble burst. Because the stock markets had resumed their growth patterns, capital was becoming more plentiful. Interest rates were manageable and attractive, and the atmosphere for real estate investing had been configured so that speed and leverage (the ability to borrow on assets) pushed the real estate markets to frenzied heights. The internet bubble (and subsequent crash) were ultimately followed by a real estate bubble.

Real estate prices were climbing rapidly — doubling in some instances — and getting much attention. But that doesn't draw a complete picture of the returns on real estate investing during those years. There were much higher returns than that. Because real estate could be purchased with as little as 10% of the purchase price put down by the investor, and borrowing the other 90%, the return on the client's investment could be substantially more. *"Hold up Dad, this is starting to get a little 'jargony.' (That's a word, isn't it? — It is now, right?!)"*

Ok, let's assume a fictitious woman, Mary, bought a modest Cape Cod house for $100,000 by putting up an initial investment (i.e., down payment) of $10,000 and financing the remaining $90,000. If Mary subsequently sold the same house for $200,000 just a couple years later and repaid the lending institution the $90,000 borrowed, Mary would have gained $100,000 on her $10,000 investment. In this simple, hypothetical example, the return would have been tenfold — 1,000%. *"Oh, WOW! Dad — that's beating the bank guarantee!"*

YES, the real estate markets were climbing rapidly! As the lending for the real estate purchases increased, the quality of those purchases was put under greater review by the federal government. Just as it was for stocks, real estate prices were outperforming their under-lying values — and, in some cases, ridiculously so. This review put increased pressures on the lending institutions to maintain better and higher funding levels. But it also resulted in low-performing and poorly financed assets being sold — sometimes with great cost (and loss) to the home owners and real estate investors.

Earlier in this book, I stated that I stayed away from debt because it could accelerate real losses. It was no different for real estate invest-ments. To the contrary. It was much, much worse. Let's talk about the second investor (we'll call him Bill), who bought the Cape Cod house from Mary for $200,000. He put $20,000 down and borrowed $180,000. Bill was put in a difficult position when the market value of the house was reviewed and reassessed at $150,000 a short time after he bought it. *"Uh-oh Dad, that doesn't sound good!"*

Because his loan was for $180,000, Bill might need to put more capital up as collateral for the property. His original $20,000 was wiped out. The bank now had a $180,000 loan on a property that was only thought to be worth $150,000. Bill would need give the bank more money to pay down the loan to the value of the house, at the very least. This was money that Bill might not get back if there were other problems and if he ultimately needed to sell the house. *"WOW! Sucks to be Bill, right Dad?"*

If Bill couldn't (or wouldn't) put up the additional capital, the bank could institute their **foreclosure** process. (This is where it gets ugly.) To limit the bank's continued or future losses, the bank might then have sold the foreclosed property quickly — at an even lower price — say $100,000.

 Foreclosure: The financial institution legally takes over the property to satisfy the outstanding debt owed.

So, by banking rules and laws, the bank would have to write off the difference between the loan amount ($180,000) and the foreclosed sales proceeds ($100,000) plus Bill's deposit ($20,000). That's a real loss of $60,000 — not a perceived loss. So, if you're keeping score at home, Bill invested $20,000 — lost that — and now technically owes the bank $60,000 more for a house he doesn't own any more. Bill's got problems! (This stuff really happened — to many, many people and institutions.)

It happened so completely, quickly and with regularity that some lending institutions couldn't maintain the proper capital requirements and were forced to close. It also meant that capital necessary for corporations to operate became much harder to get. As those companies struggled and faltered, it put pressure on even more companies with whom they dealt. Once one set of companies went out of business or shed employees, it affected other companies. Entire businesses eroded. The former employees could no longer maintain their payments on their homes or real estate purchases they had made, and their homes were sold — again, sometimes at losses. Quickly, the real estate problems escalated. (Again, from the third chapter and our pebble in a pond rippling the water analogy — somebody dropped a meteor three times larger than the pond, onto the pond.) *"Ok Dad, I get that there can be outside distractions — some that I might create and some that the world creates. But specifically, how does that affect the time aspect of investing?"*

Time didn't change, but how we worked with it already had. Because we had an investment statement and plan for investing, we didn't need to create or change our plans. While other people were spending time trying to figure out what to do and how to do it, we were already hard at work looking for bargains and making investments. Because we spent the time thinking about and evaluating our investment plans, we didn't need to use precious time trying to create one in a quick moment. Our investment philosophy statements were not going to change. We had resisted using debt to over-leverage our wealth. We didn't have the same kind of real losses to try to make up. We were focused on what we wanted to accomplish and diligent in our pursuit. We spent less time worrying about our investments and very little time (comparatively) on trying to figure out what to do next. When others were scurrying for time, we weren't.

Because my clients and I had spent so much time talking at our initial meetings together, it afforded me opportunities to gain time elsewhere. My goal had been to have one or more long meetings at the beginning of our journey together, so we would need fewer meetings readdressing fears and backtracking the way the portfolio was structured. Using large, well-recognized investments was another way we saved time. I spent less time explaining what the business did. The companies' own branding efforts served us well. When clients were worried, their fears were addressed quickly and easily as we refocused on how the company operated and how their business might have been impacted. In short, I spent less time defending the companies, but the clients saved even more time because they spent less time worrying about their investments. They rested more peacefully knowing that the companies they owned shares of would continue to serve the population, despite what the markets might be trying to say.

There were other subtle ways to gain or lose time. Throughout this book and from early in my career, I've tried to convey my investment philosophy statement using common stock and company references. At their core, they are the easiest for most people to understand. Expressing things in these terms saved us time. The strategies we used were the same when we invested in bonds; however, the bond markets are not as widely recognized or understood. Most other investment products either stem from stocks and bonds or can be reasonably compared to them, so understanding individual securities seemed to me like the lowest common denominator.

When clients didn't want to engage in the selection and decisions associated with owning individual securities, we looked for other alternatives — typically, mutual funds. Similarly, for clients with limited funds, and for those who wanted exposure to other types of investments (whether growth-oriented or otherwise), we would turn to "packaged" products, which provided them with professional selection and management in most cases. In very few instances, when the client preferred, indexes or other auto-pilot products might have been used.

At those times, the initial meetings might have been a little shorter and overall time was saved — if the client's understanding of the product(s) was high enough during troubled markets or economic times. However, these products would also conjure up other questions about who makes the decisions, who bears the risks and how the costs to clients are impacted. (In our next chapter, we're going to talk about how we want to live and deal with distractions. That's different from just recognizing and trying to limit them.)

My intention was to become as little of a distraction to them as possible. In this regard, we would be moving with time, and with strong efforts to limit when and how we would go backward. Because we had spent time up front thinking and learning, we moved more quickly and efficiently. Understanding how my practice was structured and operated then became a very important aspect, as it affected their investment strategy. It pulled in one of the last things I think you really should think about as you begin investing — *how do you want to live?*

? **Something to Ponder After Chapter 6:** Do we invest some time before we put our money to work, or do we invest our money and then put in some time for it to work? Perhaps these questions might make you wonder what would happen if you invested more time and more money.

Dollars and Sense

Young Adults:

Have you ever been given "the look?" Yes, the look! You know, the look that your parents or grandparents or a teacher gave you when you've just said something that you shouldn't. The look that sits you down and puts you in a quiet mode? In a split second, in time less than it takes to utter one word, the looker has communicated a message to you. Maybe it's a stranger who has shot you the look and frozen you — because you recognized it as "a look like the look." At these instances, you're moving in nanoseconds. In short, you're operating with very little time.

But those quick, reflex reactions that you're applying weren't developed instantaneously. They started with that first "No!" you received as a toddler. Throughout the years, you learned to interpret the "No" with the proper look. A "No, no, no" delivered with a broad, toothy grin wasn't the same as the furrowed brow, stone-faced, grimacing "NO!" you'd seen before. You had spent years learning and discerning the look.

As we age, we all move faster because of what we've learned. There was a time when you couldn't recognize these letters or their sequencing into these words. Scoff at that? What if that sentence was written this way: Было время, когда вы не могли распознать эти буквы или их последовательность в этих словах. It might take you a little while to translate this from Russian, without a Russian-English dictionary or your friend Google Translate.

(continued)

Because we all want to move faster, do things faster and live faster, we often want to "cut to the chase" and just get to the end. With my lifetime of investment experience — as a professional — my best advice to you is to invest a little time trying to learn to be successful before investing your money. That's the best way to avoid getting ripped off or doing something dumb with your money. But the good news is, with your influencers and this book, you're doing exactly that. Congratulations! Well done.

P.S. One more thought on this. Investing time isn't a one-way street. Your company might be investing money in you via the benefits they provide, but it's best that you understand where they invest time in you, too. There may be classes or learning modules. They may have dedicated meetings. They may provide other resources. They are investing in you. When you sit down with a financial professional, they should be doing the same thing, as well. They should willingly invest time with you as you hire and engage them. If not, maybe they aren't as good with investments as you need them to be. (I'm just saying.)

Influencers:

I guess, like many before me, I must be getting older. I've gotten to the point in my life where I've started paying attention to time. Maybe it comes with middle-age (which I'm determined to push back another twenty years into my mid 70s). Ancient philosophers and noted scholars pondered time. Modern physicists continue to study time. We all want more of it — yet some wish to speed it up to do more with it, and others wish to slow it down to preserve and savor it.

In all my years of school, I never took a class in time. I studied mathematics, English, history, civics, business, law, music, religion — but never time. Maybe, had I taken physics, I might have had an introduction to time study. But alas, I didn't.

"Learning earlier" is what this book is about. But as I hope you can tell, it's not about learning the rules of retirement accounts or the effects of tax changes. It's about building trust and understanding risk(s), recognizing the difference between logic and emotion, understanding math in application and dealing with time — and just a few more things in the final two chapters that await you.

But this chapter was about time. Earlier in the book, I mentioned time and the power of compounding. I've chronicled my time and learning and done so on very dramatic backdrops of extremely good investing times and very difficult and trying (OK — lousy) investment periods. Ironically, some of the best investing times were when the markets were struggling and some of the hardest times were at the market tops. It is my goal with this chapter to encourage young adults and first-time investors to consider investing time before investing their money.

Likewise, from my perspective, if young investors invest earlier, they'll save time later and have more time to do all the other things they might want. That's right, I'm hoping to do both: speed it up to do more and slow it down to savor it. I'm guessing their multitasking, amped-up, wonderfully talented generation really isn't that different from all those generations that have come before. They just have faster and cooler tools — and a new book to help them.

CHAPTER 7

So Dad, you said, 'In our next chapter, we're going to talk about how we want to live and deal with distractions. That's different from just recognizing and trying to limit them.' Well, this is the next chapter; what did you mean?

"I like being busy and juggling a lot of things at the same time. I get bored easily, so I need to do a lot."

– Ellen DeGeneres

"BUSY-NESS"

How you handle distractions is up to you. You can try to avoid them, or limit them, but what ultimately happens is your decision. Your involvement in your financial future is a big part of how things will work — but this part can sometimes get lost when you first sit down with your pro(s). Because you don't know what to do or expect (and because the financial advisors know you're new to this), many times, the pros will dictate how you interact with them.

I remember hearing, many years ago, about another consultant who put an egg timer in his office and used it to make sure that he was efficient with his calls. With that, he could press to make even more calls and do more things. He blocked his schedule and instructed everyone around him to never disturb him unless something was literally on fire. He wanted "No Distractions." If someone were to call him, they would need to leave a message (at first with his assistant, and later with his voicemail). He would get back with them during his blocked-out, "call-back" time slots on his calendar.

That's not how I approached my practice. There wasn't just one constant speed or rhythm to each day, week, month or season. I tried to be available and responsive as quickly as possible and would work calls in between calls and appointments. Many times, the caller was surprised when I first answered the phone. When that wasn't possible, my assistants would try to help the clients and prospects as much as they could. The goal was to provide exceptional customer service where no person should wait for help or answers. In contrast to that other consultant, we would process distractions and still stay focused on the things that were important to us and to the people who were important to us. But being responsive wasn't the only priority of the office.

Performance was very important to us, but not more important than compassion, understanding and dedication.

In 2003, when the Ellen DeGeneres Show first aired, it emphasized wholesomeness, acceptance and kindness (and still does). This is a great example of how I ran my practice. My focus on those values was directed much more toward helping the clients than just pure performance of their accounts. Sure, performance was very important to both of us, but not more important than compassion, understanding and dedication. There was a lot more to the practice than just designing portfolios, making commissions and having smooth, normal days.

In the early years, the Christmas holiday season was our busiest time. Building a call list, cold-calling prospects, asking probing questions, delivering the presentation, and checking in and following up with customers were interrupted. Addressing holiday cards, picking out and delivering gifts for select customers, making last-minute gifts of securities, and piecing together year-end portfolio evaluations would squeeze their way into our schedules. This created even more distractions for everyone to process. Think about how much busier *you* get during the holidays. Your decorations, shopping, baking, special parties, friends and relatives all squeeze into your busy world — maybe even more things pop up that need your attention.

Immediately after the winter holidays, tax season had us tracking down IRS forms. Piecing together income sources, researching the cost basis for securities sold, and preparing both long-term and short-term capital gains and loss statements became daily activities. We had to prepare value statements for the gifts made to charities and gather other tax information to be used by the tax preparers. In some cases, this meant meeting the client at their bank to make a list of their holdings. We'd also have to check to make sure that none of the securities were on dividend reinvestment or held someplace else. During those periods, it was so busy that reading news and researching ideas seemed to occupy the very last row of seats on a crowded 747, back there with the lavatory, engine noise, the flight attendants and drink carts. Everyone seemed distracted in the spring.

Most of these services could have been performed by the clients themselves — if they had had the knowledge, time and inclination to do so. For me, however, these were the valuable services we offered as a full-service securities **firm** and the reasons the clients

Firm: There are many types of financial service firms. Some offer a full range of services. Some only handle transactions and don't give advice. Some offer complex financial models, and some just handle packaged products (e.g., mutual funds, index funds or insurance products).

There are different fee structures for different services. There are even more specific types of investment companies. Banks and insurance companies perform both similar and different services, too. My firm was a full-service firm that either charged higher commissions for transactions or fees for other services. Understanding what type of company that you are working with and how they are compensated are great early questions you might ask.

would pay higher commissions when buying or selling securities. If they hadn't needed our help, they could have set up an account with a discount brokerage firm at a cheaper cost. Performing these services was where I thrived. So, like Ellen, I liked being busy and juggling a lot of things. *"Sounds a bit chaotic, Dad."* More than you can imagine.

In the middle of all this wholesomeness, I was also an institutional trader and worked with a multibillion-dollar pension. The institution dealt with many firms, and we were just one of them, and as busy as my day might have otherwise been, when they called, time twisted. The rest of the day was put on hold as I switched into trader mode. *Talk about being distracted from whatever else I was doing!* My focus and attention would become trained acutely on a lone security or, in rare instances, a couple of securities. Performance on many thousands of shares was measured in fractions of dollars — carried to five decimal places, to be exact. Any error could have cost thousands of dollars. The distraction of the day would consume me. *"OK Dad, why are you telling me this?"*

Just like you and like my clients, I approached each day balancing the ways in which I was going to do my job despite the distractions of the day — whether the interruption was delivered by the marketplace, the management of our firm, my personal life, other clients or the institution(s). Because we were acting on long-term plans, we'd maintain long-term focus. As I had to figure out how to deal with my distractions, I had to help my clients deal with theirs. More importantly, I had to be very careful whenever it was necessary for *me* to become the interruption or distraction in their lives. *"So, what's the big deal with this, Dad?"*

Well, that other consultant wanted no distractions in his practice. There's nothing wrong with that approach and, in fact, many efficiency experts might agree that his method was key to increased productivity. But that's not how I was wired. I liked the distractions and learned to work with them. Those will be issues for you to think about, too.

Do you mind distractions and feel a lot like the other consultant who wanted no distractions and engineered his day around avoiding them? Remember, they can affect time — but as we discussed in the previous chapter, some distractions might actually save time down the road. Are you at the other end of the spectrum, and even love and welcome them? If you want to surf, do you want your professional to call you whenever they spot a possible ride or to say that it's time to get off the wave and look for something else? Or would you prefer to be sent an email setting up an afterhours appointment — or maybe schedule lunch together?

Maybe you'd rather schedule a regular monthly call and just address things at those points in your life. Maybe monthly is too frequent. Are you fine with your mutual funds and money managers controlling things? You might only want to talk with them once or twice a year, unless something comes up or there's a specific need. This is relevant because you play a big part in how your professional relationship will develop. You and your advisor need to fit together and, just like I said above, there's a lot more that the pro does behind the scenes than you may have thought about.

WHAT WERE WE HIRED TO DO?

My practice existed to help my clients with their investment needs and build wealth over their lifetimes. I understood that, as busy as my world was, their lives were just as busy — if not even more so! Typically, their lives left very little room for them to survey the interest rate environment, pay attention to the national economic data and employment trends, or analyze an emerging technology trend. At the very least, they didn't want or need to worry about *an additional* something else. But, in rare instances, some of them liked trying to do those very things.

Over the course of my career, my practice and the industry shifted from a transaction-oriented sales practice to one that concentrated more squarely on advice. While I had shifted early in my career toward holistic advice, my compensation remained commission based. I was compensated only on the pieces of the portfolios that were adjusted and when trades were executed. I operated this way throughout my career for the benefit of my clients.

In my opinion, it offered investors the most reasonable method of investing. I felt it gave them the most control over all aspects of their account(s). I felt our being focused on generating the cash flow from which we could build, the clients had all the choices regarding what to do with their excess cash. They could use it to pay their mortgage, for a vacation home, or even for some other type of real estate venture. They could give the excess cash flow to their children, grandchildren, friends, charities, or could let it pile up some and reinvest it when the times were right ... if they wished.

But here's an important thing for you to consider — they controlled the decisions about who would select the securities — and how much it cost. For many clients, they controlled what they bought, sold and the related tax ramifications — I just made recommendations. Because these decisions only impacted the securities that were being considered, this system provided them a very efficient method of acquiring and adjusting securities. The investors chose how to build their wealth and how involved they wanted to be in handling the investment of their savings, retirement accounts, education planning and children's funds. Ultimately, they would decide how to pass the accumulated wealth onto their beneficiaries at their death(s). Again, those decisions will be yours, too. You will decide if you make the decisions or leave them to your trusted advisor or relinquish them to another specialized, financial professional you and/or your advisor select.

As you can see, my system was designed to maintain that decision-making with the client — for the most part. When the client wanted to be more growth-oriented or wanted to consider alternative or foreign securities, we may have opted to use a mutual fund instead of individual selections. This gave them professional selection and management. In those cases, we gave away control and accepted the outcomes of the fund managers' decisions. We gave up control of when sales were made and lived with the gains and losses the managers effected. Shifting control to the professionals cost more for the clients than my model, but it was their decision to do so. This decision was also used by many investors with limited resources. It provided them with diversification, because owning just a few individual securities might expose them to more risks than they could tolerate.

Many financial consultants had opted to move to a fee-based practice, where quarterly cash amounts (based upon the value of the accounts on specific days) were deducted from the accounts. Typically, the more removed the client wanted to be in the process, the lower their control of actions within the account went — and the higher the fee-structure would go. This deduction of fees was "real" negative performance, not just a perceived event. Regardless of whether the account went up, down or sideways with perceived performance, it would be going backward on a real, regularly scheduled time. Granted, very few people wanted to pay charges when their accounts were down, but the charts in this book have shown there were indeed times where that was happening. Taking money out of an account that was down meant that they went just a little further backward at those times.

For many, shifting the control freed up their time and gave them peace of mind that a knowledgeable professional was working for their best interest.

But understand — for many, shifting the control freed up their time and gave them peace of mind that a knowledgeable professional was working for their best interest. That's something you should think about, too. If you're first starting and don't have much to manage, mutual funds and certain packaged products might be something to consider to spread out the risks of owning a single stock or bond (or just a few individual securities).

And understand this, it isn't all or none, now and forever. *"What do you mean by that, Dad?"* Well, not everyone starts paying attention to their investments when they're young. Some might not really look at them until they're retirement age. Others might inherit money and/or securities when they've older. Some people want the professionals to take over because their wealth is greater than they think they can or want to manage themselves. But other people need their money managed for them because they don't have the physical or mental abilities to do it themselves. What would have happened if Romanoff had died while he was still taking care of Beatrice? She might have needed their banker or other financial professional to take care of her. People change. Needs and preferences change. How you work with your professionals can change. And, of course, these changes in your world can be distracting to how you operate.

People change. Needs and preferences change. How you work with your professionals can change.

So, as I had to decide how to work with my distractions, I also had to learn how to work with my clients when I knew that I would become a distraction to them. My clients, on the other hand, chose when and how they could be distracted. For example, I had a wonderful client named Helen. Helen was in her late 70s and gave strict instructions never to call her before 11:00 a.m., unless it was an emergency. She was a night owl and liked to stay up late reading the *Wall Street Journal* while watching *The Tonight Show with Johnny Carson* and other late-night TV shows. She'd then sleep in and stroll slowly through her morning. Another woman, slightly older than Helen, liked to swim in the early morning — 5:30 a.m. to be exact — before her YMCA got too busy. She wanted to get a jump on her day. I would try to never call her in the mid-afternoon because that was when she liked to nap.

Other clients had different preferences, and it was my job to know them. Some wanted to meet at their homes. I generally preferred to meet at my office but would try to accommodate their wishes whenever possible. Some lived in different states that had different time zones than mine. Some lived part of the year in one state, and other parts of the year in another. We all had to learn how to adjust.

> **"We are very much a microwave society. People don't want to wait."**[1]
>
> *– Rick Pitino, NCAA Hall of Fame Basketball Coach*

As a society, we tend to want everything instantly. To society, success can be measured in seconds and fractions thereof. Did I win the lottery last night? How many times has my Tweet been retweeted? For many, investment returns are no different, and surfing on the edge to build wealth requires millisecond reflexes, and a professional approach. Even then, clients are not assured of positive results. For many, pressing for even higher returns meant paying higher fees for the latest emerging ideas and theories. The pressures to perform on the short-term basis were costly.

"Hang on there, Dad, this is starting to feel like that Ricky Bobby story of speed again." Good catch. You're right! (See, you are learning.)

---

1   http://www.cardchronicle.com/2015/10/29/9621470/
     rick-pitino-and-the-evolution-of-the-microwave-society

My goal was *not* to beat an index or see how great a return could
have been gotten in any lone year. Going back to why the clients
had come to me, for most, it wasn't their goal either. Their goal was
to get a better return than the banks were willing to guarantee them
given a certain level of risk over a defined period — and that period
generally had become their lifetime. Working with a pension gave me
a much broader perspective to investments. *"Why's that, Dad?"*

Pensions are older types of retirement programs typically set up
by large companies, as well as state and federal agencies, for their
employees. The pensions take in contributions from the employers
while the employee works there. The pension then promises to pay
out benefits, which will begin at a later date and continue for the rest
of the employee's life (and sometimes beyond, to their heirs). The
contribution period might have begun when the employee got out
of high school or college and continued until they retired at a much
older age. Those assets would be invested to grow and produce benefits that not only would begin at a much later date, they would also
need to plan for inflation (the increases in prices we pay for goods
and services.) To prepare for investing over such long periods, the
pension hired companies to calculate the performance of all types
of investments and prepare reports to help them take care of the
employees. The good news for me was that they published the results
of the calculations as they set their goals. So, I knew the long-term
results they were seeking and their general methodology for
investing. But again, they were investing for thousands of employees
collectively and using general population assumptions.

While much simplified, my methodology followed many of the
lessons their research revealed. They balanced risk, return and
cost. So did I! They monitored and maintained a relatively low turn-
over rate (how often they sold what they had purchased earlier) to
keep cost low and improve performance efficiency. So did I! They

approached investments logically and without emotion, and limited distractions to their investment approach. While they might have been fortunate to generate spectacular returns at times — because that was what the markets generated - they were never materially concerned with a microwave (instant) approach to investing. I was indeed fortunate to learn from them and used that knowledge for the benefit of my clients (and now for you, too).

Instead of worrying about short-term performance, I focused on the long-term design of portfolios. I helped with the construction of the "house" and the selection of the "bricks." I stood ready to serve my clients. I tried to be quiet until needed — not adding to the noise — but loud when needed to be. I was ready to alert clients of an opportunity that fit them or if there was a notable risk or problem. Of course, I was also always available to them to answer any questions that came up or when life got in their way and they needed our help.

Together, we had learned how to handle our distractions and live the ways we wanted. This will be important for you to work out with your financial advisor. It should be handled with respect and compassion on both sides of the relationship. If your advisor can't respect how you want to live, you'll have a problem. And if you don't like how they operate their practice as it affects your life, I'd suggest that you talk to another professional, too. Maybe there's another way to handle things, or possibly you should re-consider what you expect. But remember, you're the one who's paying the professional. You have rights, and they should respect you.

If your advisor can't respect how you want to live, you'll have a problem.

---

*"So Dad, I think I get it now. I need to have an idea of what I'm trying
to do. When I sit down with the HR people or the pro, I need to build
some trust with them and see how we fit. Then, we'll come up with
a little bit of a plan to set me up. You gave me some other things to
think about — like, how much of a shopper or surfer am I? Why are
we buying what it is that we're buying, and why would we want to
sell it later? Do I understand the math and going backward: real or
otherwise? And we went through quite a bit about trying not to get
distracted and how to handle distractions when they pop up. I also
get it — if I start earlier, I'll probably do better in the long run. But do
I really need a big plan of what to do for the next 40-60 years? I'm just
starting out. How elaborate of a plan do I need? I barely know what
concert is coming in town next month. And what happens if something
comes up, like I lose my job or have an accident?"*

Great questions and issues. You have been paying attention. Midway
through my career, I questioned and thought deeply about the role of
financial planning within my practice. Because the role of the consultant was taking a more holistic approach toward investing, many of
them were trying to increase their understanding of a wider array of
products. The professionals and institutions were trying to adjust and
control their portfolios to hopefully provide more consistent, predictable returns. It meant they could better prepare for the needs of the
population in general.

Understanding the general needs of populations is very important
to investing, but for my individual clients, I tailored my advice
much more specifically to each of them. When they could retire
was not a theoretical question. Death of a spouse did not generally
occur specifically on the average life expectancy chart. Marriages,
jobs, accidents, and childbirths were never done in the vacuum of
"average." They were much more personal.

My clients' specific heredity came into question. If "35.3% of deaths in American women over the age of 20, or more than 432,000, are caused by cardiovascular disease each year,"[2] when should that have been factored into their specific financial plan — during the next economic growth period or the next recession? As much as I might have related those statistical averages to the plans, their personal preferences to risk also came into play. Were they cautious and concerned about their investments — but not as concerned about their health — or vice-versa? Had they really planned to coincide or correlate to the performance of the S&P 500? Did they *plan* that their investment returns would look like this chart?

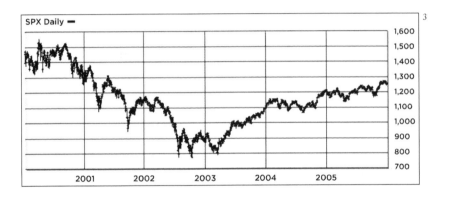

Did it correlate to their children's weddings, graduations, grandchildren's births, divorces, illnesses or job changes?

At times, we might have been tempted to ask, "If we used all the most sophisticated research and data, and planned accordingly, why didn't the markets follow our plan?" Ultimately, these questions led to predicting the markets, economy, interest rates, and life events for

---

2   https://www.cardiosmart.org/heart-basics/cvd-stats

3   S&P 500, 12/31/1999-12/31/2005, http://bigcharts.marketwatch.com

immediate or short-term results and decisions. Short-term planning tended to have the opposite approach from what I wanted. It pulled many of the old questions I wanted to avoid back into consideration: What was controlling our actions? Greed? Or fear? Were we getting sucked into the *emotion* of the markets versus the *logic* of the markets?

With the trillions of dollars invested in the various types of equity and debt markets, it was easiest to think of them collectively as oceans in which we were attempting to swim. Oceans have their own natural traits: relative temperatures, stream patterns, tempos, ecosystems and the like. The markets did too. Did a sunny day at a specific beach truly indicate what was happening in the ocean? Did the storm that rocked the cruise ship spell trouble for the ocean? Likewise, did a strong day/week/year indicate the true health of the markets? Did the decline of the Dow Jones Industrial Average mean there were troubles within our companies? Did the actions of the day cause me to shift my focus from playing offense to becoming defensive? Was I focused on building wealth through buying, or had I become defensive when times were troubled and I was trying to protect my portfolios during the storm?

With the trillions of dollars invested in the various types of equity and debt markets, it was easiest to think of them collectively as oceans in which we were attempting to swim.

"Wait, Dad ... are we going through all that risk and trust stuff again?"
No. But see what happens when we get a little distracted? It sneaks in and pulls us through the same old questions and issues. But this time,

you caught it. You didn't want me to get distracted and go through it again. Look who's taking charge of the investment conversation! You're not sounding nearly as scared or confused now. That pitch isn't going to whizz by you in the HR batter's box (or the financial pro's client seat) without you noticing it anymore.

For me, the questions of financial planning were best served by trying to build a system that had a higher probability of building wealth with each client. My focus remained centered on maintaining cash and cash flow, reducing taxes and controlling costs, and buying securities at what we believed were discounts to their worth and holding them until they were fully valued or trading at a premium. Our efforts were focused on trying to build incomes and real returns. We tried to stay in control of what we were doing. We were logically trying to buy low and sell higher. We tried when the markets were at their lowest — after the crash in 1987 — after the dot-com bubble burst — after 9/11 — after the Great Recession — and at every high point between and after, too.

"Great Dad, why don't I just cut to the chase and follow your system and use your stuff, if it worked so well?" It did work well and still does for many people. But other financial consultants have their own strategies and are equally successful, if not more so — perhaps. The world of investing is constantly changing and evolving. More people are participating today than ever before. It was just how I operated; not a statement or criticism on how anyone else managed or should manage their practices.

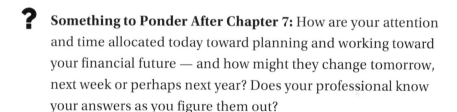

The world of investing is constantly changing and evolving. More people are participating today than ever before.

Together, my clients and I had a philosophy that guided us. But we also had developed an understanding of one last insight — the one that carried us through those highs and lows and soothed us during the times in between. I think it will help you, too, and wrap up this conversation about building and handling wealth. That last insight is what I like to think of as the art of financial consulting.

? **Something to Ponder After Chapter 7:** How are your attention and time allocated today toward planning and working toward your financial future — and how might they change tomorrow, next week or perhaps next year? Does your professional know your answers as you figure them out?

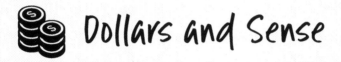

Dollars and Sense

Young Adults:

So, how are we doing? If my chapters had simple titles, I might have called this one "Spring Break." Spring break is a grand time of the year — when school is almost over, most all the hard work has been done, and there's just a tad more learning to do before we set out for the next grade, level or adventure. (OK, there's a few parties that week that you might not want to miss, but remember my first advice — Don't Drink Anything Blue.)

This book is almost over and look at the transformation that you've gone through. Maybe you started with fear of getting ripped off, doing something dumb, or of not being taken seriously or respected. Now how do you feel? You're more knowledgeable. You've been thinking about this subject a little while now, and while you may not have the answers to all your questions, you certainly should be less scared to ask them. Maybe you've started creating a bit of a plan for yourself or know a little more about what you want to do.

Spring break always marks something else, too. You aren't really in the same grade anymore. If you had started the year as a college freshman or first-year service member, you're now much closer to be a sophomore or second-year member than you were — much older and wiser than just a few months (or pages) ago. And just like that, you're not as much of a young adult as you were when you started this book. But this isn't high school anymore, and you're no kid. Instead of grey-haired folks dictating how everything works, you're now at a spot to begin working with the pros and laying out how you want to do things.

This chapter was about stating for yourself how you want to live. You determine how distractions will be handled in your life. You can do things to avoid them, and you will determine when and how you address them. You determine how much control you want to maintain in the investment process and, together with your professional, you'll figure out what you want and need to know. If you want to jump on this topic of investing, then jump on it. If you'd prefer to rely on others, that's your choice, too. There's no right or wrong answer — only your answer. And note that throughout your life, these answers might change, too.

But alas, spring break is over, and we must trudge off for just a little more learning before our time is finished. (Gee, spring break just flew by — doesn't it always?!) But don't fret, this level of schooling is just about done.

Influencers:

This is the day that you've hoped for and dreaded in so many ways. Well, not actually today, but this time of life. As influencers, we strive to help our young adults and first-time investors get to the point where they truly start taking control of their lives and making wise decisions on their own.

Sure, they may have already moved out of the nest, but so often at the first sign of something new, the call comes. Once again, we're needed to provide the advice or reassurance they're seeking. This book isn't an attempt to replace the call, but rather is my attempt to help you and them address their

(continued)

issues together — instead of you just doing it for them. And that's really what this chapter was about.

Up until this chapter, I/we were still in the "here's some things to think about" mode. This chapter was the beginning of the exploration of how they want to do things. You might think it's a little bit of a dangerous chapter because it focuses on their choices — which might not match with how you operate. (I'm sure this is the very first time you've had such differences with them — ha!). Hopefully, the foundation of underlying thought has been set, and now you can begin having a true discussion with them.

And this is really where the important part comes in! Your discussion and input will be an integral part of their knowledge and mindset when they sit down with the investment professional or HR person. You'll go into the meeting with them whether you're physically there or not. But, the real difference is now they are more educated and have given some thought to the subject. Sure, they'll still have questions, but those will come more from lack of experience than lack of knowledge. Or perhaps, they might just come from lack of confidence. That's the subject of the final chapter, and the point at which I completely turn them back to you.

Dangerous — that's the term I used above. Not because either you or they might make mistakes, but because this might be where you start to differ. But differing isn't bad. It's neither right, nor wrong. It's not where mistakes really are made. They're just different points of view and perhaps the spot where your wisdom shines through once more (like when you gave them a great book to get them thinking about these things).

CHAPTER 8

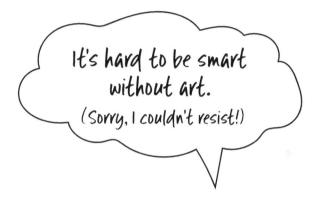

"The noblest pleasure is the joy of understanding."

– Leonardo da Vinci

While most famous for creating the paintings *The Last Supper* and *Mona Lisa*, the famed artist was also a sculptor, an inventor, a scientist, an engineer, and a mathematician. Da Vinci studied art, nature, science, mathematics, and logic (among other things) and noted their interconnectedness. Similarly, building an investment portfolio is more than just math, probability, science and psychology.

Throughout this book, we've talked about the psychology of investing — confronting our emotions of fear and greed with logic. You were pressed to think about time — starting earlier and the benefits of limiting or controlling the distractions that effect time. We studied a few basic math facts and began trying to apply engineered thoughts to building wealth. We discussed the general nature of society, and you were encouraged to think of how that relates to you specifically — your wants, needs, preferences and decisions. But investing money and building wealth involve more than math, psychology, sociology and science. There is an art to working with investments, too.

Investing money and building wealth involve more than math, psychology, sociology and science. There is an art to working with investments, too.

It's a form of art to which each person can individually and personally relate — and it's an art form that constantly changes. The products change. Their owners' (investors') needs can change. The laws that govern their environment change, as do their results and measurements. The owners themselves change as the portfolios are passed or given to other beneficiaries. There is an art to investing. *"So Dad, you're saying that art is important in business? You always hear of the starving artists — not the savvy business-minded artist. What does art have to do with building my retirement account and wealth?"*

> **"My body is my journal, and my tattoos are my story."**
>
> *– Johnny Depp*

Sitting in a shopping mall today, one sees art everywhere: in the designs of cell phones, shoes, clothes and store signage. Even the brands of the items are forms of art, both separate and integral to the products themselves. What connected a music storage device and cell phone now also connects TVs and a form of payment — all united through the art of a piece of fruit with a missing bite. The art of today arrives in tattoos, phone designs, architecture, t-shirts and brands.

Art is ever present in commerce, in business and in wealth building. Personal wealth is a different form of personal art. It may be built by and for one individual and yet may not match or fit the needs of the next owner. But you and your friends know all about art in today's world because of the prevalence of tattoos.

Tattoos are some of the most personal forms of art an individual can own. They can be so truly unique that only the owner knows their meaning. It might be a specific date, name, character or caricature. The body art might have universal symbolism, like a religious symbol or the peace symbol. It might be both, where "Mother" is specific to the owner but evokes thoughts by the onlookers about their own mothers. Tattoos may be publicly displayed across the hands for all to see, discreetly hidden under clothing or positioned in a spot that could be either private or public, depending on the owner's mood. *"Yeah Dad, but what do art and tattoos have to do with investments?"*

OK, let me help you out with this a little. At the end of this sentence, close your eyes for a few moments and picture the investment tree on the corner that we talked about earlier in this book. Now in your mind, you had a picture of a tree. Was it an oak tree, a pine tree, a palm tree or weeping willow, perhaps? Did it really matter for our story? No, but the tree in your mind was your tree. So, imagine now that you're back in kindergarten and your teacher said to the class, "I want you to take out a piece of paper and color me a picture of your tree." You pulled out your crayons and started drawing away. Maybe your tree had a purple trunk and yellow leaves. Why? Perhaps it was because purple was your favorite color, or your brown crayon was broken. Wasn't it still a tree? Weren't you creating your picture the way you could and wanted?

OK, now at the end of this sentence, close your eyes and picture the house you want to build someday. Did your house have a roof? Was it pointy or flat? Did your house have a front door? How about windows? OK, all these images are images of traits in many types of houses, but they're also components of office buildings, castles and hospitals. And even though they all have many of the same or similar components, they are all very different and unique.

OK, one last time, at the end of this sentence close your eyes and think about the investment portfolio that you want to draw/build. *"Wait a minute there, Dad! I don't have any idea how to draw that picture."*

OK, so your think of your financial professional as your own sketch artist, who will help you design your portfolio. You tell them what to put in your picture. Maybe you want some surfing investments because you like excitement and can handle wild rides. Maybe you want environmentally protective investments because protecting the planet is very important to you. You start telling your sketch artist how to draw your portfolio/house. *"So how do I do that with HR at work?"*

When you go into the HR office, and sit down to start sketching out your portfolio, tell them that you like to surf or that you don't like to lose money. Ask them what they can predict and how certain are they of those predictions for you specifically. Depending on the plan that they offer, the HR representative will help you start drawing up your financial picture. Now, that person may only have big, fat, Crayola 8-pack crayons to work with. Their investment tools might be limited, but they can still help you draw you a pretty good house.

If you have other money, you can sit down with a financial consultant. They might have the 64-pack of crayons, or colored pencils, or oil paints. They might be able to draw the intricate design of the little plate that goes around the doorbell of your house. And again, your house might be very different from the kid's in the next seat. They both have roofs, doors, windows, etc. but remember your house is yours and fits you at this moment, and his house is his and fits him. By now, you should have a few ideas of what you want to draw — an investment seed for your first tree, or maybe the shape of your first investment house.

Throughout my career, I worked with my clients and helped them with their art. Maybe I started with them as the sketch artist, and later transitioned into their art teacher. To some, I became their art colleague. Looking back across my nearly three decades of experience, I think about all my great artist clients. Some looked very similar, and others quite different, but in general they had evolved just as you have. Your ability to draw might have changed greatly since kindergarten, or not. But now you know what you like and what suits you. The same was true for my clients.

By the end of my career, the clients generally expressed less worry about their investments than when I had started my career. Their diversified, properly weighted portfolios were producing predictable incomes and tax effects. They were in better control of their fees and expenses. They learned that patience, time, and logic can mend little mistakes and make up ground — if the mistakes were, in fact, little in nature. They refrained from acting out of boredom and were more disciplined when they were buying and/or selling their securities. In those boring, flat times, they were getting paid while they waited. They were building cash reserves to be used when bargains were presented. Instead of letting fear and greed take hold of them, they were discerning between facts and logic. They avoided the impulse to hop from one horse to what was hopefully a faster horse. If it was thought to be a good horse, they just added it to their stable and continued building.

They constantly assessed how they wanted to be wrong and whether they were being lucky, smart or some of both. They understood those differences, and we were humble enough to admit which. We could also admit when we had made mistakes. They protected their wealth when they were lucky and took advantage when they could be smart. They tended to stay away from debt, betting, junk products and speculation. While each of them had personalized portfolios, and many of them had similar security positions, each was in fact unique.

> **"If your lifeguard duties were as good as your singing, a lot of people would be drowning."**
>
> *– Simon Cowell*

Television talent-show judge Simon Cowell has made a name for himself being critical. In each of his shows he expressed his opinion as to the talent level he thought the contestant possessed. Sometimes his opinions matched those of the other judges. Sometimes they didn't. Sometimes he seemed blunt in his assessment, or even perhaps rude. For some people, his criticism challenged their skill level. For others, he challenged their readiness to compete. Many artists long for such criticism. They want to be challenged to be better. While winning the show's competition was certainly a worthy goal, it was not the sole measurement of each contestant's success. Indeed, many non-winners were better because of Cowell's critical judgements. And even when the judge didn't care for the performance, it was an expression of the contestant's art, nonetheless.

In like fashion, I was once fired by a client because my approach was too simplistic for his wife. While she claimed to know nothing about investing, my shopping analogy offended her. She felt that I did not respect her advanced degree and ability to understand complex theories.

Occasionally, a few other prospects I met along the way just wanted results. They didn't care how they were produced. They chased returns and shopped methodologies when they became dissatisfied with the performance. They spent time and money complaining and suing consultants because they didn't get what they thought or hoped they'd receive. I didn't allow them to become clients of mine and referred them elsewhere. They had no time for all my talking, rules, opinions and lessons.

"OK Dad, is that it?"

Almost. There are two more points that I want to share with you — the last two before we're finished. The first point is that you should remember, everyone has their own reasons for doing what they do. While you might be tempted to copy from your neighbor's paper, be very careful. On the same day that one of my clients was adding to their XYZ stock position because it was thought to be undervalued and offered a unique opportunity for them, my next appointment might have been selling his shares in the same company, on my advice. It might have been that they needed the money, and this security had the least negative tax consequence for them. This happens a lot more than you think. It happens every day, all day. For a stock to trade, there must be a buyer and a seller. Each has his or her own reasons for doing what they do.

And the last point is this — your financial professional can't legally or ethically tell you what they, themselves, do — and they shouldn't. For the very reasons I just pointed out, they shouldn't because your circumstances are different from theirs. If they bought XYZ and then told you to follow them, they are potentially guilty of what is known as "front-running." They can't put their needs or wants ahead of yours — to get better pricing, to affect their returns or to use it as persuasion. Just because they bought it, or sold it, has nothing to do with whether the security is attractively priced or fits your needs. *"Wow Dad, thanks, but is that how you want to end this? There's been a lot in this book. Can't you pull it all together for us, so we know what to do?"*

OK, here goes. This is neither a "how-to" book nor a rule book. This is my expression of how I practiced my art as a financial consultant for 27 years. Over that time, I created and tested my investment philosophy statement. It was what I believed, and how I approached (and continue to approach) my investments. Below is my investment philosophy statement summarized:

1. I invest money to attempt to get a better rate of return than the bank is willing to guarantee (given a certain level of risk) over a defined period. I am a long-term investor and the period is my lifetime. I am very much a value-oriented investor, and from that perspective there are only three levels at which a security can trade: at fair value, at a discount-to-fair value or at a premium-to-fair value. I spend most of my time trying to identify the range of fair value for a security. My intentions are to buy them when they trade at a discount to that range and hold them until they trade at fair value or a premium-to-fair value. I want to invest in only the best (or second best) companies in their industries. They are proven leaders and have real earnings.

2. I believe that growth is a perceived return. It must be converted to cash or something that produces cash to become a real return. To build wealth over time, cash and cash flow are needed — because we build wealth buying things, and we protect wealth by selling them.

3. I only sell a security because I need the money, because there is a significant change in the operation or management of the company that changes it into something different from what I originally bought, or if there has been a rapid, appreciable rise in the price of a security over a relatively short period of time. As carefully and deliberately as positions are added or expanded in my portfolios, so too is the discipline used in selling or reducing them. I resist surfing for returns or trading for faster horses.

4. I believe in diversification and moderation and want to focus on the things that I can most likely control with a high degree of probability — income and taxes. I try to assess how I might be wrong and avoid going backward in real returns. This includes limiting taxes, fees and expenses as best as possible. I resist the temptation to borrow money to make investments for short-term performance.

I believe successful investing takes time, patience and discipline.

---

5. I believe successful investing takes time, patience and discipline. I resist letting short-term distractions, fads or pressures push me into investing for different purposes, such as beating another security, index, market or even just trying to get back to even. When I don't know what to do, I wait until it becomes clearer before acting. I go with what I know and not with what I hope. I focus on building returns, not chasing them. And lastly ...

6. I believe that this is *not* the best, truest, most efficient way to build wealth. It is what worked well for me and my clients throughout my career. Investments change. Markets change. The

rules that govern both change. I believe that continually trying to challenge and improve my investment philosophy statement will ultimately create a better philosophy statement and process.

If asked, "How does one paint?" what would da Vinci have said? Does it begin with picking up a brush or finding an inspiration? If asked about the *Mona Lisa*, what would he say he was trying to convey: Simplicity? Melancholy? Grace? Beauty? Through nearly three decades of my career, I worked with each of my clients to address their personal desires, tolerances and emotions. They were painting their pictures the ways they wanted. It was just my approach to investments that they tried to follow.

The methods of this book and my rules toward investing should be debated. This is art. It fits some, but not all. It worked and continues to work, but are there better forms or fashions? The purpose of this book is to urge you as — individuals, students, and young service members — to begin building what you believe at an earlier age. Just as I questioned my investing methods over time, tested other theories, and refined (and revised) them, so should you. Like da Vinci, I believe you should try to separate the art, science, mathematics, and logic of finance and delve into their interconnectedness.

This is where the role of the advisor or consultant comes into play My role was to advise my clients on the actions I thought they should take to achieve the true objectives they sought. That was the initial reason they came to me and my dad — even if they didn't know it. That was why I entered the profession and remained — not to have been a salesperson who cashes in on commissions — but to help my clients and prospects develop an understanding of investments and attempt to build wealth that could last a lifetime. To me, that was the role of the financial consultant.

This book was designed to challenge you.

- Why are you investing?

- What are you trying to accomplish?

- How do you want to operate?

- What are your opinions on risk and trust?

- How much of a shopper, surfer or something else are you?

- Do you have rules or methods for achieving your desired outcomes?

- Do you just buy securities because you have extra money, or are you building something specific and looking for pieces at designated price levels?

- Do you maintain focus in a world of distractions?

- Is emotion taking over your decisions, or are you logical in your thinking?

- Are discussions of your wealth distractions in and of themselves?

- Have you considered the costs and how much control over the investment process you want?

- When you sit down with an investment professional, are you working together to meet your goals in the manner best suited for you?

From my experience, the sooner you consider these questions, the more likely you will be moving toward building wealth to last a lifetime.

"Thanks for your help Dad, I love you." You're most welcome. Now go on out there and jump into the financial batter's box and get a hit. Or head off to the financial fish market — you won't be coming home with an octopus and telling me the great deal you got on this crazy kind of fish. Love you, too.

? **Something to Ponder After Chapter 8:** Is your future financial picture drawn with invisible ink, stick figures, brilliant colors or something more abstract? Is it something you want to start drawing yourself, or would you like to have a sketch artist do it for you? However you go about it, when it's all said and done, it's yours to keep.

"Teachers open the door. You enter by yourself."

  – LEARNING

"You've got to be very careful if you don't know where you are going, because you might not get there."

  – DIRECTION

"It's because it's what you love, Ricky. It is who you were born to be. And here you sit, thinking. Well, Ricky Bobby is not a thinker. Ricky Bobby is a driver. He is a doer. And that's what you need to do. You don't need to think. You need to drive. You need speed. You need to go out there, and you need to rev your engine. You need to fire it up. You need to grab a hold of that line between speed and chaos, and you need to wrestle it to the ground like a demon cobra! And then when fear rises up in your belly, you use it. And you know that fear is powerful, because it has been there for a billion years. And it is good. And you use it. And you ride it; you ride it like a skeleton horse through the gates of hell, and you win, Ricky. You WIN! And you don't win for anybody else. You win for you, you know why? Because a man takes what he wants. He takes it all. And you're a man, aren't you? Aren't you?"

- SPEED

"If you can dream it, you can do it. Always remember that this whole thing was started by a mouse."

- DESIGN

"Life is a carousel. It goes up and down. All U gotta do is just stay on."

- PERSEVERANCE

"You may delay, but time will not." "Time is money." "Lost time is never found again."

- TIME

"I like being busy and juggling a lot of things at the same time. I get bored easily, so I need to do a lot."

- FOCUS

"The noblest pleasure is the joy of understanding."

- ART

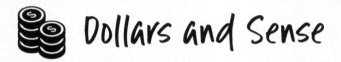

Dollars and Sense

Young Adults:

Well, we made it. Here we sit at the back of the book, and our chat together is finished. I was thinking about you very specifically when I wrote the second to the last paragraph of this chapter. I was thinking of how you might have approached those questions had I put them at the beginning of the book versus just a few moments ago. The difference in my mind is that you now face them more confidently and perhaps with a bit more logic.

Confidence — it is, indeed, a powerful tool. If you don't have very much confidence, you can get stuck while you try to muster the courage, or figure things out. You might stand while everyone else dances, or sit the bench when others get to play. You may be overlooked for a promotion while your less skilled colleague advances. But, too much confidence can have its own problems.

Too much confidence can have you rush so fast that you trip or fly wildly out of bounds. There's a fine line between being over-confident and arrogant. There aren't many people who like dealing with arrogant people. More importantly, arrogant people aren't cut much slack when times get tough. And there will be a time that you'll hope that your boss, spouse, kids, friends, relatives, neighbors — somebody/anybody — cuts you some slack as you work through your difficulties, whatever they are.

But my goal when writing this book was to help you get in the game — to dance — to be successful — to build some confidence about a subject with which you probably hadn't had much experience yet. You've now been coached what to do. Stroll in and get to work — and know that I'm rooting for you and proud of what you've accomplished. You're going to do great. Be confident!

Influencers:

This is the point where there is but one last thing that I must say to you. I must say Thank You — to each of you — with all sincerity and as much respect as I can possibly offer.

Thank you for granting me the opportunity to share a few of my thoughts (OK, maybe a smidge more than a few, but who's counting?) with those young people you love, support and influence. I earnestly hope that I produced a quality tool that will help them, you and some of the institutions that shape them. I thank you for taking the time to review this book; and for sharing it with them if you thought it (or even just parts of it) appropriate, useful and beneficial.

Thank you for indulging my attempts at humor and for being patient as I twisted through some spots to make a point. Thank you for trusting me with young men and women so precious to you and allowing me to try to help them. While I wished them well and told them of my pride for what they've accomplished here, I should also say how grateful I am that they have terrific influencers who care for them and want to help them succeed. If not for you, where would they be or go? Congratulations and be proud, too. They're better because of you.

Glossary

B

Bank Run: After the crash in 1929, banks were swarmed by customers demanding their deposits be returned to them. They feared the bank would fail and run out of money, and their savings would be lost. *16*

Bond: A debt, issued by a corporation or government entity, that paid interest and was to be re-paid to the owner at a specific date in the future. Think of a corporate or government IOU with interest. *27*

C

Capital Gains Taxes: The Federal and most State governments require that taxes be paid when securities are sold at a profit. The amount owed is calculated as a percentage of the gain. Each state has its own policy on taxes. *108*

Capital Intensive: Requiring much money to secure land and/or rights of way and construct the infrastructure to operate the company's mission. *42*

Certificate of Deposit (CD): A bank-guaranteed product that promises to pay the holder a specific rate of interest over a specific period and then return the original amount invested back to the holder on a set date. *20*

Cold-Call: An unsolicited call to an unknown potential client, also known as a prospect. *14*

Commission Sales: No salary or fee. Compensation is determined by a % of sales. *14*

Credit Risks: The risk that the companies or government agencies could act in ways to hurt their ability to repay their debts. *26*

Currency Risks: The risk that the exchange rates of currency between countries changes to negatively affect the current holder. *26*

D

Default of Payment: The buyer of a security refuses to make payment for the security purchased. *56*

Divesture: Some companies own some (or all) of other companies. Rather than continue to own the shares or sell them, they could just give them to their current shareholders. Then the shareholders would have two companies to keep or sell as they pleased. *64*

Dow Jones Industrial Average: A fixed collection of companies thought to generally represent the industrial aspects of the United States. *15*

F

Financial Markets: Central places where securities are traded. *17*

Firm: There are many types of financial service firms. Some offer a full range of services. Some only handle transactions and don't give advice. Some offer complex financial models, and some just handle packaged products. *140*

Foreclosure: The financial institution legally takes over the property to satisfy the outstanding debt owed. *129*

I

Inflation: A continuing rise in the price of goods and services generally attributable to the growth in demand for them. *39*

Inflation Risks: The risk that prices of goods and services would increase. *26*

Interest Rate Risks: The risk that the interest rates would increase, making current products less valuable. *26*

Investment Philosophy Statement: A written description of what you believe about investments and how you want to operate. *37*

Investments: Financial products of various types (also known as securities) *11*

M

Market Risks: The risk that the entire market would decline. *26*

Maturities: The stated length of time a CD, bond or other debt security will last. *35*

Mutual Fund: A collection of investments that are professionally managed for a specific purpose and are publicly traded within a financial market. *23*

P

Political Risks: The risk that the foreign governments would act in ways to de-value their own country's investment products. *26*

Portfolio: A specific, complete collection of investments. *64*

S

Securities Firm: A company that buys, sells and manages investments for clientele. *14*

Shares/Stocks: Transferrable units of ownership in a company. For this book, generally traded publicly at various markets. *27*

Splits: Some companies thought their stock traded better at lower prices, so they sent out many more shares and adjusted the prices after that (e.g., an owner of 1 share of a $100 stock could have been sent another share and then have 2 shares at $50). *64*

Stock Dividends: Instead of sending owners earnings in the form of cash, they delivered more shares of stock (e.g., 5% additional shares – if you owned 100 shares, they sent you 5 more). *64*

U

Utility(ies): A company that provides a community with electricity, natural gas, water or sewerage services. *27*

V

Volatility: Quick, unpredictable and meaningful movements. *83*

About the Author

A FINAL MESSAGE FROM WES RUTLEDGE

For most of my adult life, I've juggled four vocations at the same time. I had a professional life as a financial consultant and trader with a regional investment firm. My second vocation started as my way to network and give back within my community and resulted in my moving up the chain within a large civic organization. I went from passing out t-shirts all the way up into the board room and ultimately served as the Chairman of the Board. — *And did I mention that it had 75 civic leaders as board members and that the organization entertains 1.5 million people annually?* — My third vocation was/is as a husband — a very, very lucky husband — who has a wonderful wife who put up with those first two lives and let me grow and develop all those years. Together with her, we developed my fourth vocation — dad of two terrific kids who are now even better young adults.

I had been groomed for a life as an investment professional — even if I hadn't known it. My dad spent most of his life as a stockbroker. I went to business school and followed in his footsteps. Together, my wife and I began building our financial life, and after completing a great career, we had amassed financial success. Let's be a little clearer with this notion of "financial success." We're not talking about "won the lottery, gas up the jet, polish the yacht's deck" wealthy. We're talking about successful enough that I could walk away from that first life, live comfortably and spend even more time with the third and fourth vocations. Together, with my wife, I decided to expand my role as dad to see if I could help even more young adults.

I don't know if you've noticed, but none of my vocations involved becoming an author. Sure, I had learned to write for my job and my other responsibilities — but those writings were vastly different from the ways I communicated with my children. It operated, in fact, the other way around. Once I retired from the world of Wall Street, the man who took control of my practice noted how similarly the clients spoke like me. They used the same common, everyday terms. They were focused more on their lives than the world of finances, and they had a pretty strong sense of what they were trying to accomplish — and were doing so. In short, they were building their wealth in common fashions, even though they didn't necessarily know each other with a common language — my language.

Indeed, my first three vocations would set the table for taking my vocation as dad to a different level. Now, don't get me wrong. I'm not trying to parent other young adults. I'm not giving advice, nor am I telling anyone what they should do or consider. What I am attempting with this book is to share how I operated, in a language they understand, so readers can begin thinking about their financial futures and how they might want to operate themselves. There are many, many smarter and wiser people than me. What I am hoping to do with this book is to encourage their development. That's right ... I'm hoping that my vocation as a dad will help unleash many, many smarter and wiser young adults in the world of finance. And then, even more smart and wise things can be done and written. And that's what this author is really all about.

MORE ABOUT WES'S FINANCIAL CAREER

For over 27 years, Wes Rutledge served as an investment professional with the same conservative regional investment firm. With his practice, he extended his father's career, which started in 1947 when he came home from Europe after WWII; his father's career spanned more than 40 years. Wes and his dad used the same method that worked through those periods, and continues to work today.

Wes worked with hundreds of clients and helped manage millions of dollars' worth of all types of investments — conservatively over $100 million at his retirement. He worked with clients of all sizes — first-time investors with less than $20,000 to doctors and lawyers with more than $15 million per client — retirees, professionals, small business owners, corporate executives, grandparents, parents and their children. He also traded millions of dollars' worth of securities for two multi-billion-dollar pensions.

Wes's financial career started in July of 1987 — just before the worst market crash ever. He soared through the 90s with the greatest bull market ever recorded, survived and thrived through Y2K and the dot-com bubble burst and its ensuing recovery, then patiently guided clients through the Great Recession and helped them extend their success.

Having accomplished all this, together with his wife, Wes secured their family's future. He retired from the financial services industry at the end of 2014 at the age of 52 to move away from financially based performances to focus on other mission-based causes. Extending education through this book is just one of them.

Acknowledgments

Blessed! That's what this page is all about — how blessed I've been throughout the writing of this book. There are many places I could start trying to say thanks, but I must start by thanking my God for all the people who have contributed so many different services and forms of support to me. That said, let's start with my family.

To my wife, Terri, all that I am today has been complemented by you. Your patience and guidance, trust and love have not only allowed me to write this book, but was a source of inspiration for all the decisions I made. You've been my first audience member, editor, consultant and guide as I wandered this author's path. When I wasn't sure what to say, do or where to go, you were there to help me. I love you — always and forever. **To my children, Morgan and Wesley.** You're my true inspirations. I'm so proud of you both, but I'm also so glad that you both are patient enough with me to teach me. Morgan, much of the editing and questioning throughout the book was done with your help. And Wesley, your voice and reasoning kept me real and inspired in so many ways. Indeed, I am blessed to be dad to you both. **To my three older sisters and my three younger brothers**, you shared our parents with me. You helped shape me in so many ways, and as much as I carried our dad into this book, I tried hard to carry you and mom with me, too. My tone of family comes from the love I have with you. God blessed me with a terrific family!

Next on my list must be my editorial boards — yes, it says "boards." First there were a few friends who would peek at my early drafts and weigh in. That takes real friendship to look at the writings of a non-author as he tries to peck something out. While there were several, and I don't mean to slight anyone, the three most drawn upon were **Jill Bell, Mike Seebert and Greg Kuhn**. Jill, my friend since kindergarten, your support every day for the past 30 years (sure I know it's been quite a few more years that that, but we aren't that old, are we?) has been felt every single day. There's nothing we don't go through together. Mike, one of my earliest mentors and fine friend. You were with me when I first uttered "don't drink anything blue" to your young adult daughter and have been a source of wisdom and laughter throughout my career. You're a gem of a buddy! And Greg, you're a relatively new friend, but my author-mentor and now close confidant. I knew nothing about writing a book, and yet you patiently pointed me in the right directions and kept me going. My second editorial board took up the challenge of reviewing my "re-visioned" manuscript and helped me hone it into the book it is today. To **Andrew Bronger, David Johns, Angela Edlin, Teresa Kosse, Tim Long, and Rena Sharpe** — please know how much I thank you. Like my first board, each of you left your fingerprints on this book, and I'm so proud to say that it's better because of you.

To Larry Goldstein, the author of this book's foreword, your friendship and council have inspired for many years. You're such a consummate professional, terrific friend, and — above all — a man I most admire. **Greg Vincenti and Andrew Bronger**, both shaped who I was as a financial consultant. Greg — my manager, leader and captain — your leadership and guidance actually pale in contrast to your abilities to listen and care. And that says a lot because you're a terrific leader and guide. Andrew — my protégé, friend and now, my consultant — without you, I could never have made the transition from consultant to author. Your abilities to listen, care, guide, teach and take care of your clients are exemplary. Well done, my friend and thank you. This list wouldn't be complete without **Kenny Green**. Kenny was there on my first day of my career, the last day before I retired and every day in between. To be honest, I was like the pesky little brother to Kenny — the one who popped into his office to comment or chat about the markets, our families, the weather or whatever was on my mind. Greenie, nobody had a greater influence than my dad on how I practiced my profession, but you were certainly very close. For over 25 years, we sat side by side and experienced everything together. Thanks again for sharing the ride!

Lastly, without the sage advice of my literary professionals, my thoughts and intentions would lie in a wadded pile of paper or boxes of undistributed books wedged into a corner of my basement. The first pro I must thank is **Cathy Fyock, my book coach.** I showed up in your email box wondering if there was a way to advance my thoughts into a book, but not just any old book — I wanted a better book for my young adults and influencers. And that was before I had even identified those audiences. Cathy is the real deal, people! She patiently guided me to my publishing team and guided the re-visioning. Patient, did I say she was patient? She endured my *eight* different attempts to find a better tone in Chapter 1. That's great coaching! She also led me **to my publisher and editor, Kate Colbert.** Poor Kate had to take on a former investment professional and try to make him look something like an author. But that's where she excels! Together with Cathy, they took their top-tier skills and guided this puppy home. But there's more to Kate than just that. She's a very fine leader of an awesome team at Silver Tree Publishing. **Courtney Hudson**, your cover design, typesetting and artistic concepts have literally put the face on my work and fleshed out its body. And this fine, trim, young, good-looking face and body were exactly what an aging dad needed. **Penny Tate**, my project manager, without your steady guidance and constant support, I'd still be wandering my office looking for what to do next and hoping it's not past due. And before **Stephanie Feger** became my publicist, she first served as my mentor and we quickly became fast friends. You're an inspiration and a blessing.

Thanks to each one of you, and to my other family members, friends, neighbors, and constituents, and to you my audience — I am indeed very blessed to have you.

Go Beyond the Book

BE SURE TO VISIT THE OFFICIAL BOOK WEBSITE!

SoDadTheBook.com

Contact Wes at Wes@SoDadTheBook.com for bulk sales information and/or to schedule group speaking engagements.

And watch the website for other timely Wealth-Building Insights to be posted!!

A portion of the proceeds of *So Dad, How Can I Make Dollars & Sense?* will be donated to the Kentucky Derby Festival Foundation for distribution to institutions — public, nonprofit, military and other foundations — dedicated to promoting financial education and literacy for young adults.

Made in the USA
Lexington, KY
21 July 2019